THE ILIAD AND
THE ODYSSEY
TROY

Paul Demont

THE ILIAD AND THE ODYSSEY
TROY

HACHETTE
Illustrated

Introduction

14

The Iliad

16 The War without Achilles
18 The Anger of Achilles
24 The Achaean Army
30 Helen and the Old Men of Troy
36 The Feats of the Warriors
50 The Exploits of Hector
56 The Trojans Scent Victory
68 The Death of Patroclus

76 The Return of Achilles
and the Death of Hector
78 The Grief of Achilles
82 The Fury of Achilles
92 Water and Fire
100 The Death of Hector
106 The Funeral of Patroclus
112 The Plea of Priam

The Odyssey 116

The Adventures of Telemachus 118
Athene, Odysseus and Telemachus 120
Penelope and the Suitors 130
The Voyages of Telemachus 136

The Voyages of Odysseus 146
Odysseus Leaves Calypso 148
Odysseus and Nausicaa 154
Odysseus and the Cyclops 172
Circe the Magician 186
Hades 190
The Island of the Sirens 196
The Final Tests 202

The Reconquest of Ithaca 208
With Eumaeus the Swineherd 210
Odysseus Begs in His Palace 220
The Bow Test 234
The Massacre of the Suitors 238
Penelope and Odysseus 244

Characters in The Iliad and The Odyssey 250
Further Reading 252
Index 254
Photographic Credits 255

Contents

Invocations to the Muse

Sing, Goddess, of Achilles, Peleus's son,
In his stark wrath, which brought upon the Greeks
Infinite troubles, and shot on to Death
Many strong souls of heroes, whom it made
A prey to dogs and all the birds that came;
In the accomplishing of Zeus's design,
From when at first they quarrelled and they parted,
Atrides king of men, and bright Achilles.

The Iliad, Book I, lines 1–10.

O Muse, record for me the man who drew
His changeful course through wanderings not a few
After he sacked the holy town of Troy,
And saw the cities and the counsel knew
Of many men; and many a time at sea
He in his heart endured calamity,
While his own life he laboured to redeem
And bring his fellows back from jeopardy.
Yet not his fellows back from death he won,
Fain as he was to save them: who undone
By their own hearts' infatuation died,
Fools, that devoured the oxen of the Sun.
Hyperion: and therefore he the day
Of their returning homeward reft away.
Goddess, God's daughter, grant that now thereof
We too may hear, such portion as we may.

The Odyssey, Book I, lines 1–10.

Homer,
by Tamas Galambos, 1992.

Western literature began with *The Iliad* and *The Odyssey*, in the written form in which they appeared in Greece from the 9th to the 6th centuries BC. Since then they have nourished literature over the centuries, from Greek tragedies to Virgil, from Fénelon to James Joyce. The first of these epics, *The Iliad*, tells the story of some two months in the final year of the Trojan War. Troy was a city in Asia Minor, also known as Ilion (which explains the epic's title). For ten years the Achaeans, who the poet also calls Danaans or Argives (but never Greeks), confronted the Trojans and their allies. But, as the first prologue says, the poet concentrates on a single event, the anger of Achilles and its immediate consequences, and he finishes his poem when they (the deaths of many warriors, in particular of his friend Patroclus and his opponent Hector) have been worked out. However, he assumes that his audience knows the general historical framework and its outcome, the capture of Troy by the Achaeans, which the Ancients dated at 1218 or 1184 BC.

Here is the general background. Achilles is one of the many heroes who have come together under the command of Agamemnon, son of Atreus (whence his alternative name 'Atrides'), to avenge the abduction of the beautiful Helen by Prince Paris-Alexander, son of the King of Troy, Priam. They had taken an oath when Helen married Menelaus, King of Sparta and brother of Agamemnon: if someone ever tried to break up this marriage, which they had all aspired to, they would declare war on the aggressor. However, far away from Sparta, on Mount Ida in Asia Minor, Paris had had to decide a beauty competition between the three principal goddesses of Olympia, Hera, wife of Zeus, the king of the gods, Athene, a virgin and daughter of Zeus, and Aphrodite, another daughter of Zeus and goddess of Love. He judged Aphrodite to be the most beautiful because the goddess had promised him the love of Helen, the most beautiful mortal woman. Paris then had no compunction in abducting Helen from her palace in Sparta (either willingly or by force, according to different versions) and taking her to Asia Minor. We know all these events from illustrations of myths and theatrical adaptations; they were also the subject of other lost epics in what is known as the 'Trojan cycle'.

The Iliad is primarily the epic of Achilles. In the Achaean army Achilles, the son of a powerful goddess, Thetis, and the mortal Peleus (whence his name 'Pelides') is the most formidable and courageous of the heroes. Without him, the Achaeans would not have stood up to the Trojan offensives. But one catastrophe did hit the Achaean army, the plague, because Agamemnon refused to return his prisoner, the daughter of a priest of Apollo, in exchange for a ransom. Warned by a soothsayer, he finally agreed to release the girl, but on condition that Achilles handed over to him his own prisoner, the beautiful Briseis. Faced by what he saw as an unbearable insult, Achilles decided to stop fighting. His mother Thetis got Zeus to agree to avenge Pelides by preventing the Achaeans from winning the war. Zeus's plan was first to give Agamemnon false hope. The heroes were successful without Achilles but, despite several incidents, the Trojans got close to their fortifications, then to the Achaean ships, even setting fire to them. Then, in a first gesture of solidarity, despite the offence he had suffered, Achilles authorised Patroclus to put on his own armour which, by itself, would spread terror among the Trojans. But Patroclus went beyond the

The Garden of Troy,
by Samuel Bak, 1972.

orders Achilles had given him: he was recognised and killed by Hector, another son of Priam, commanding the defence of Troy. Achilles went mad with grief and, haunted by the wish to avenge Patroclus, he decided to return to the fight with new armour specially made for him by Hephaestus, the blacksmith god, all the while knowing that if he killed Hector, he would die soon after. He massacres large numbers of Trojans, then confronts and kills Hector, defiling his corpse. *The Iliad* concludes with the spectacular funeral of Patroclus, then with the return of Hector's body, which Achilles finally agrees to after meeting Priam, Hector's old father, who in turn gives his son an honourable funeral in Troy.

The rest of the story is not in *The Iliad* – the death of Achilles (killed after being wounded in the heel by an arrow) the trick of the Trojan Horse, devised by Odysseus, and the capture and sacking of the city. However, the death of Achilles is an end-point often mentioned, particularly by the hero himself and his mother Thetis:

Ah, woe is me
Unhappy mother of the best of sons!
For I have borne a matchless son and strong,
First of the brave: he shot up like a sapling;
I nursed him like a plant on a rich slope
And sent him forth in the curved ships to Troy
To war upon the Trojans; but I am
Never to greet him at his coming home.

Book XVIII, lines 54–59.

This 'scion', this young branch, will be cut down at the height of his powers: Thetis knows it, and Achilles knows it too. And when the prologue of *The Iliad*

heralds the misfortunes of the Achaeans and the deaths of *so many brave souls / Heroes* as a result of Achilles' anger, we all know that this triumph of death implies the death of the divine Achilles himself. The concern for honour assumes acceptance of the terrors of death. For although death is not annihilation, the souls of the dead lead only a sort of half-life in Hades, devoid of pleasure. What is more, death in combat and the defilement of the body often lead to disfigurement, and sometimes the bodies are no more than *food for the dogs / And birds without number*. On the other hand, when magnificent funerals are staged, they provide a final homage to the dead person, and when his deeds are eternally celebrated in epics, then death becomes almost beautiful. This is why the expectation of death, the choice of death and the account of the death had the power to charm audiences of *The Iliad*.

The Odyssey takes place after the Fall of Troy, and is also mainly devoted to one hero, Odysseus, who is mentioned in the prologue. A reading of the two prologues immediately shows that *The Odyssey* is a very different work, almost the exact opposite. The perspective of *The Iliad* is death, that of *The Odyssey* is life, and even, at first, survival. Achilles chooses to fight and die out of his concern for glory; Odysseus, having taken Troy with his trick, uses all his inventive powers to escape death in all the extraordinary places he goes to, from Troy to Ithaca. The death of all his companions, for which the poet immediately absolves him of all responsibility, enhances his own successes, and the companions' 'fury' (or madness) highlights his wisdom.

The first part of the poem focuses on Telemachus, and Odysseus is only mentioned indirectly. It describes the son's voyages in search of his father. In his homeland, the island of Ithaca, he and his mother Penelope are horribly threatened by the group of Suitors: these local lords feast endlessly in Odysseus's palace, insolently stripping it of its riches and hoping to win the hand of Penelope and the throne of Odysseus. On the advice of the goddess Athene, Telemachus decides to leave Ithaca. In Pylos he meets old Nestor, then in Sparta he stays with Menelaus and Helen, who had been back there for a long time. These heroes of the Trojan War describe their own adventures, particularly the taking of Troy, as well as the part Odysseus played in it, and the difficult return journeys of the Achaeans, tragic in the case of Agamemnon, who was assassinated in Argos by his wife Clytemnestra and her lover. The story of Agamemnon and Clytemnestra provides a kind of background for the return of Odysseus, for whom Penelope patiently waits. The return of Odysseus is the subject of the second part of the epic. The initial stage follows him from the island of Calypso to Phaeacia. For seven years the hero has been a prisoner of the nymph Calypso, who would like to keep him forever in her wonderful cave, and sleeps with him every night:

But therewithin Odysseus high of heart
He found not then; who, sitting far apart
On the sea-beach, as oftentimes before,
Fretted with tears and sighs and bitter smart.
Book V, lines 81–83.

Zeus, at the request of Athene, Odysseus's regular protectress, orders Calypso to release him, and so Odysseus manages to reach the island of the Phaeacians on a raft he built for himself, despite a dreadful storm sent by Poseidon, the god of the Sea. There he is welcomed by Nausicaa, the daughter of King Alcinous, who also wants to marry him. Now Odysseus describes his earlier adventures to Alcinous, from the capture of Troy up to his arrival on Calypso's island. As he explains, he had to deal in turn with the Cicones, the Lotus-eaters, the Cyclopes, the god Aeolus, the Laestrygonians, Circe, the Sirens, Charybdis and Scylla, losing companions along the way, before the last of them died through their own fault for feasting on the cattle of 'the High One', the Sun, who saw to it that they never returned home. He even went down to Hades to speak to the dead. After these famous descriptions, the Phaeacians agree to take him back to Ithaca. The third part of the story takes up the second half of the epic, and tells how Odysseus and Telemachus win back power in Ithaca. They meet outside the city at the hut of their faithful servant Eumaeus, the swineherd. Odysseus withholds his identity, except to his son, and disguises himself as a beggar to get into his palace incognito. Only his old dog, that no-one looks after, recognises him, and then dies. Odysseus puts up with the snubs of the Suitors, and even has to have a fist-fight with a real beggar before he wins the right to take part in the Test of the Bow, to decide which of the Suitors will be Penelope's future husband. This is when he reveals his identity and takes his revenge. The fight starts: Odysseus and Telemachus triumph with the help of Athene, massacring· the Suitors and punishing disloyal servants and unfaithful serving women. Then Penelope learns of Odysseus's identity, but makes him undergo a final test before she takes him to their conjugal bed. Finally, Odysseus visits his old father, Laertes; then Zeus and Athene impose a reconciliation with the inhabitants of Ithaca which puts an end, perhaps for ever, to the trials of the hero.

Sing, Goddess ... O Muse, record for me ...
Who is this 'goddess' or this 'muse' from whom the prologues of both epics request a song? The request is repeated later in *The Iliad*:

Now tell me, Muses, on Olympus dwelling,
(For goddesses ye are, and present ever,
And know all things, whereas at best we hear
An old tale and know nothing) ...
Book II, lines 484–486.

In the first lines of *The Odyssey*, who is the first person ('record for me') who later becomes a plural ('we too')? The author or authors seem to be associating themselves in some way with their audience, asking for something that comes from elsewhere, from the world of the gods, the song and the story, as if they were not responsible for them.

In Ancient Greece, a world where many gods were worshipped, which the poet Hesiod described and to some extent organised in his *Theogony*, the nine Muses were the daughters of Zeus and the goddess Memory. In nine successive nights, Zeus conceived these goddesses 'who help people to forget their sorrows and relieve their fears'. From Zeus, the Muses take their prescriptive and educational functions. From Memory, their function as go-betweens to bring the past to life, and as dispensers of future glory. But the setting of standards, the accounts of high deeds celebrating heroes, are above all a pleasure thanks to the Muses, even the supreme pleasure. Odysseus maintains this himself, saying to the Phaeacians before he begins his story:

Goodly it is to listen to such song
As now for our delight the minstrel woke;
Whose voice is like a god's own voice to hear;
Since no joy truly I account more dear
Than when a people all keep festival,
And in the palace banqueters make cheer,
And listening to a minstrel sit arow,
By tables groaning meat and bread below,
While, passing down, the cup-bearer with wine
Poured from the bowl makes each man's cup to flow.
No more than this I deem may man desire.
The Odyssey, Book IX, lines 3–11.

Odysseus does not mention the Muses or the Muse here, but 'a minstrel', someone often called a 'bard'. That would be a more apt description for the person at the beginning of the poem. Like the bards described in the poem (Phemius in Ithaca and Demodocus in Phaeacia), the poet of *The Iliad* and *The Odyssey* sings of the anger of Achilles and the return of Odysseus because the Muses inspire him to charm his audience. The bard is both completely dependent on the Muse, who in some way possesses and inspires him, and free to choose his own songs. This may seems paradoxical, but we need to remember that epics were produced in a very different way from writing a book in the silence of a study. Bards in Homer's time gave a kind of public performance, partly a recitation and partly improvised, singing or chanting a story about a well-known subject belonging to one of the different epic cycles. At the end of the 19th century, when bards were found in Central Europe and Africa who could improvise in verse for hours around traditional heroic themes, to a musical accompaniment, this was seen as proof of how the early epic storytellers operated. Ismael Kadare, in his novel

The File on H, wrote very well about the Serbo-Croatian *guslari* and the American academics researching them.

It is also interesting to see how people moved from these oral production methods, which were so varied, complex and free in their original phrasing, to producing written texts. This is something which since Antiquity has been known as 'the Homeric question'. Studies of Mycenean Greek, which dates from the 2nd millennium BC, and comparisons with other Indo-European languages show that 'epic diction', as the epic's phrasing style is often referred to, goes back to a very early stage in the Greek language, before the alphabet that we know was invented around the 8th century, and that it was handed down over the centuries from this very remote era to the Archaic period. At the other end of the chain, it is generally agreed that the written texts of our two epics were fixed in a first official version, probably in Athens, during the 6th century, before reaching its present state in the Hellenistic period in the great libraries of Alexandria and elsewhere. Between these two main events, it seems that one or rather two poets composed *The Iliad* and *The Odyssey*, probably around the 8th century, with or without the help of writing, working from previous accounts. Before the researches of the 'oralists' (who believed that epics had wholly oral origins), the philologists had been divided since Antiquity into the 'unitarians', who believed in one author, and the 'separatists', who believed there were many authors. From the 17th century, studies of the Ancients relaunched the debate. The Romantics wanted to find primitive bards at the root of the 'official' version, authentic representatives of popular poetry. *The Odyssey* was thus sometimes carved up as people hunted for the oldest part of it, which was generally thought to be the 'Stories Told to Alcinous'. Homer's name was not invented by the Moderns, however: it definitely appeared in the 6th century, and perhaps earlier, in a fragment attributed to Hesiod. The historian Herodotus dates him to the 9th century. His existence and his role as author of *The Iliad* and *The Odyssey* do not seem to have been contested during the Classical period.

Ancient traditions state that he was blind, like the bard Demodocus in *The Odyssey* and soothsayers such as the famous Tiresias. A blind man does not see ordinary life, his vision reaches inside to the truth; he reveals the past, the present and the future. This is why for centuries Homer has been *the teacher of Greece*, according to Plato's famous description in his *Republic*, despite the philosopher's criticisms.

Paul Demont

The Iliad
Death and Glory

The War without
Achilles

AFTER AGAMEMNON, SON OF ATREUS, HAS TAKEN
BRISEIS PRISONER, ACHILLES WITHDRAWS FROM THE
FIGHT. ZEUS AVENGES HIM BY FAVOURING THE TROJANS.

*Why hath he assembled / And led an army here, this son of Atreus? /
Why, was it not for fine-haired Helen's sake? / Are Atreus's sons alone of living men /
To love their wives? No, every good sound man / Loveth his own and cares for her, as I — /
I also, loved mine own with all my heart, / Though she was but the captive of my spear.*
Book IX, lines 338–343.

But Peleus's son, his anger unabated,
Again assailed Atrides savagely:
'Wine-sodden, dog in eye and doe at heart,
Thou never yet dared to arm thyself
And lead the host to battle, nor to share
The risks of ambush with our bravest men:
That seems like death to thee! Much pleasanter
To range the wide cantonment of the Greeks
And sequestrate the prize of any man
Who dare oppose thee – folk-devouring king,
That rulest feeble people! Otherwise
This outrage, son of Atreus, were thy last.
Lo, I will say my say, and swear thereto
A solemn oath. Yea, by this staff of mine,
Which never more shall put out leaf or shoot
Since first it left its stem upon the hills,
Nor yet grow green again, because the axe
Has stripped its leaves and bark – and now the sons
Of the Achaeans, those who sit in judgment
And guard traditions by command of Zeus,
They bear it in their hands – so shall it be
A potent oath to thee: the day shall come
When all the sons of the Achaeans will
Long for Achilles: and in that day thou
In thy distress shalt have no strength to help,
When multitudes fall dying at the hands
Of slaughtering Hector. Thou shalt eat thy heart
Within thee, for remorse that thou didst slight
The noblest of the Achaeans.'

Book I, lines 225–244.

The Anger of Achilles

Achilles' Prediction

ACHILLES' ANGER, AFTER AGAMEMNON HAD OFFENDED HIM, is the human echo of a divine anger, that of the god Apollo, who was also offended. Apollo's priest Chryses had offered Agamemnon a generous sum to recover his daughter Chryseis, now a prisoner handed over to Agamemnon as part of his spoils of war. The latter had arrogantly rejected the offer, leaving Chryses no option but to appeal to his god. Apollo had listened to Chryses's plea and, with his bow, had dispatched a plague of arrows on the Achaean army. *The pyres of dead burned endlessly, in their hundreds.*

Achilles called a meeting of warriors to find a way of appeasing Apollo. At these Homeric gatherings, only the main characters played an active part. Just before they spoke, they seized the sceptre, the decorative staff which the herald passed to them and which gave them authority and symbolised the duties of justice. The prophet Calchas then explained the reasons behind Apollo's attack and the nature of his demands.

Agamemnon refused to return the girl unless he was given some other part of the spoils, which Achilles thought could best be achieved by capturing Troy. Agamemnon responded furiously, demanding that Achilles bring him the prize he really wanted, Briseis: *to prove to thee / How much I am above thee, that another / May be afraid to boast himself my peer / And match me to my face.* At this point, Achilles would have killed King Agamemnon if the goddesses Hera and Athene had not restrained him. Erupting with anger, he declared in a great speech that the Achaeans *would die in their thousands.* It is left to the reader to imagine what the inevitable result of his withdrawal from combat would be. While the poet does not allow him a particularly explicit declaration, this is because the enormous number of deaths will also be the consequence of Zeus's support for Achilles, which his mother Thetis begged him for. The king of the gods promised to prevent the Achaeans from harming him and to find *a way of honouring Achilles / And by the Achaean ships take many lives.* The action in the epic always develops on a divine and a human level at the same time, without human responsibility being diminished as a result. Thus we have an offended father trying to recover his daughter who is avenged by Apollo, then an offended son whose mother intercedes for him and is avenged by Zeus. The king of the gods punishes the king of kings. The unleashing of the war, in the final year of the conflict, will be worse than the worst of scourges, nothing less than a plague.

PAGES 14–15
The heroes of *The Iliad* did not fight on horseback, but this red-figured vase clearly conveys the heroic spirit of the battle.

PAGE 17
Meeting of the Greek heroes at Troy (scene painted on a red-figured skyphos, or drinking cup, by the painter from Brygos, one of the most famous at the beginning of the 5th century).

PAGE 19
The anger of Achilles, shown just as he is about to draw his sword on Agamemnon, is evoked through the vigour of the lines and the expressions.

OPPOSITE
Achilles dressed as a knight says goodbye to his lady, Briseis. In the Middle Ages, Homer was known only through Latin translations and Virgil. In France, the *Roman de Troie* adapted him to the world of chivalry, modernising the setting and the postures to suit notions of courtly love. The same process can be seen, much later, in this panel painted during the Italian renaissance.

Honour

No solution is or can be found to this conflict of honour. Honour is the fundamental value in Homeric society. The restoration of honour defines everyone's place in society, especially those of the 'heroes', 'leaders' and 'kings', and the 'noblest' (the *aristoi*). While they recognise the primacy of one of their number, which seems to guarantee their power (that of Agamemnon in the Achaean world, and of Zeus in the divine world), they all jealously defend their privileges. A serious assault on their honour implicates not only the offended person and the aggressor, it questions the world order.

The kings are aware that the honours they have received – *Places of honour, fine meats and goblets always full, and their immense estates / Rich in plantations as in land for the plough* – must be paid for by bravery in combat. One of them, King Sarpedon, specifically says this: *This all means we must give an example [...] / And be first to fling ourselves into ardent battle.* By treating Agamemnon as a coward and profiteer, Achilles touches him to the heart. Aristocratic society could see itself being wrecked.

> ... For my mother Thetis tells me,
> The white-foot goddess, that two diverse fates
> Are carrying me toward the goal of death.
> If fighting round the city of the Trojans
> I tarry here, goodbye to my return,
> But never shall my glory die: and if
> I do go home to my dear native land,
> Then I have lost fair fame, but length of days
> I shall have, and the end of death will not
> Come quick on me.

Book IX, lines 410–416.

Achilles is *the most valiant of the Achaeans*. He is the son of a goddess whom, according to legend, Zeus would have married if he had not been afraid of siring a son who was stronger than himself. That is why Thetis married Peleus. From his birth onwards, Achilles represented the supreme example of a man confined to remain a mortal although the best fitted to surpass this condition. For him, glory would be won by death.

OPPOSITE
Hector, Menelaus, Agamemnon and Achilles in a Flemish tapestry, 15th century. The Achaean and Trojan names provide a prestigious background to the pomp of these 15th-century lords.

OVERLEAF
On this 5th-century black-figured Attic lekane, a type of large bowl, the artist describes the final battle for the capture of Troy in a style close to that of the Corinthian artists. The hoplite soldiers are grouped, shoulder to shoulder, in a phalanx, a close-fighting technique that began to appear around Homer's time, and depended on each man protecting his neighbour.

PAGES 26–27
Agamemnon and Achilles lead the fight against Hector in the fourth battle of Troy (painting c. 1465).

... As raging fire
Burns a vast forest on the mountain tops,
And far off shows the blaze, so as they marched,
The dazzle of the innumerable arms
Went flashing through the ether up to heaven.
And as the many tribes of winged fowl,
Geese, cranes, or long-necked swans, fly all about
The Asian meadow by Cayster's streams,
Exulting in their pinions; with a clang
The van keeps lighting, and the mead resounds:
So forth from ships and huts the many tribes
Of warriors poured into Scamander's plain:
And 'neath the tramp of men and horse the earth
Rang grimly. In Scamander's flowery mead
They stood, unnumbered as the leaves and flowers
In summer. Or as tribes of busy flies
That buzz about the cattle-byres in spring,
When pails are wet with milk, so numberless
Stood the long-haired Achaeans upon the plain
And faced the Trojans, in a fierce resolve
To rend them.

Book II, lines 455–473.

The Achaean Army

Illustration for *The Iliad* by John Michael
Rysbrack (1694–1770). In France, Mme
Dacier's translation (1699 and 1708)
fiercely defended the Ancients against
the Moderns, and had a profound influence
in the 18th century.

ZEUS DECEIVED AGAMEMNON when he promised him victory. The king thought he would test his troops' morale by pretending to prepare for a return to their country: but the men reacted with such enthusiasm that it took all Odysseus's cunning and authority to get them back on the right road. Preparations for war began. Before cataloguing the different contingents among the Achaeans and Trojans, the poet describes the Achaean army in a series of majestic similes. The use of similes is one of the characteristic aspects of the epic style, and they are widely employed in *The Iliad*, which contains several hundred. As the poet himself said:

That multitude I could not tell nor name, Not though I had ten mouths, a tongue in each.

The simile is one of the poet's instruments for describing such a vast crowd of men, building the scene into a spectacle. It can produce an infinite variety of effects, modifying the point of view, as focusing is called by cinematographers, with an ease and freedom that is beyond cinema. When the army is likened to a forest on fire *on the mountain tops*, as seen from a great distance, it takes on a cosmic vastness. Conversely, a simile can shrink this mass of men by comparing them with *tribes of busy flies* or *the leaves and flowers in summer*, so that this horde of warriors are successively threatening and swirling about, as seen from inside the cloud of flies, and beautiful like the flowery meadows they are crossing. In these instances they are viewed from so high up that the point of view is almost that of the gods. Such similes have another advantage: they remove the reader from the fighting. The war is always there in the background, but the description of it advances by means of images which are largely autonomous and remove the reader from the immediate scene. We are successively confronted with a mountain on fire, then in Lydia we are in the midst of a vast flock of birds, and finally in a sheepfold during milking. The worlds of peace and nature are thus invoked at the heart of *The Iliad*, at the very moment when war and death are being described. This widening of the descriptive range is one of the wonders of the poem. Similes are not only used to describe crowds. They also have a distinctive value, as can be seen in the text that follows. At one moment it distinguishes the Achaeans from the Trojans, then (as occurs more often) it throws the heroism of this or that valiant soldier into relief against a crowded background, or as he faces his opponent. In this way the poet assembles a whole bestiary of, in part, stereotypes: wild boars, wolves and birds of prey are described out hunting and gripped in merciless combat, to point up the savagery that man resorts to in battle. Comparisons with lions are particularly frequent and varied.

Now Priam and those around him, Panthous,
Thymoetes, Lampus, Clytius, Hicetaon,
Of Ares' lineage, and the two wise men,
Antenor and Ucalegon, were sitting,
Elders in council, at the Scaean Gate;
Too old for active service, but good speakers,
Like crickets in the wood that perch on trees
And sound a thin sweet note. So on the tower
The Trojan leaders sat. And when they looked
On Helen coming towards the tower, they said
With winged words to one another softly:
'Small blame that for a woman such as this
Trojans and armed Achaeans should be bearing
Calamity so long; for she to look at
Is wondrous like the immortal goddesses.
But even so – for all her beauty – let her
Depart upon the ships, nor be left here
To ruin us and after us our sons.'
So did they say; but Priam called to Helen:
'Come here, dear child, and sit in front of me
To see thy former husband and thy kin
And friends. I find no fault at all with thee;
I hold the gods to blame, who roused against me
This tragic warfare of the Achaeans.'

Book III, lines 146–165.

Helen
and the Old Men of Troy

PREVIOUS PAGE
Helen on the Ramparts of Troy,
G. Moreau (1826–1898).
The painter conveys the terrible
mystery of Helen's beauty in a
style close to Symbolism.

ABOVE
Helen at the Scaean Gate,
G. Moreau. The Gate,
located in the west of
Troy, overlooked the plain
where the fighting took place.

The Beautiful Helen

THE DESCRIPTION OF THE ACHAEAN ARMY makes us think battle will begin, but this is deferred for two Books. First, the armies organised a head-to-head combat between the two principals, Menelaus, Helen's husband, and his rival Paris. This duel would decide the whole conflict. Helen then left her residence in Troy and went up to the ramparts to watch.

At first, we see her through the eyes of the old men of Troy, who are both wise men and gossips. In the famous comparison with crickets there is all the sun of a Greek summer. It precisely evokes the mood of immobility, dryness, infinite chirruping and warm siesta. The old men say what is not usually said, that is, that Helen, who is both guilty and innocent at the same time, incarnates the seductive power of female beauty over men, and the evils that result from it. Agamemnon and Achilles quarrelled verbally over Briseis. In Helen's case, they think it is even worth the trouble of going to war, but it would still be better if she went away. Helen regards herself as a *bitch* who would rather have been driven to suicide than have to leave her private chambers. But Priam talks to her affectionately. This hesitant, ambivalent behaviour is characteristic, providing much ammunition for later writers whose views varied between condemnation and the *Encomium of Helen* (the title of two pamphlets by Gorgias and Isocrates). As a way of exonerating Helen from responsibility, later poets even invented the story of her phantom, said to have been sent to Troy while the real Helen was entrusted to the guards of the king of Egypt (this is the story of Euripedes' *Helen*).

The Power of Love

As they stood on the ramparts of Troy, Helen pointed out to Priam the principal Achaean leaders, her brother-in-law Agamemnon, who *looks a king*, the *astute* Odysseus, *skilled in all the tricks of strategy*, and *huge Ajax, bulwark of the Achaeans*. Here she is acting as the poet's helper, to whom she seems related by virtue of her charm, introducing the characters on his behalf. Curiosity replaces animosity, and all seem to think that the end of the war is near. But the anticipated duel does not take place as expected. Paris-Alexander had only accepted single combat after being admonished by Hector, who called him a *handsome and debauched betrayer*, to which Paris replied that he should not blame *the lovely gifts of golden Aphrodite, which are the rich gift of gods and surely not to be discarded*. When they eventually fought, Paris the lover was unable to overcome Menelaus, the legitimate husband. Menelaus was on the point of killing Paris, when Aphrodite intervened to save her protégé, whisking him away from the battlefield – *a simple feat for an immortal* – and setting him down *in his sweet-scented, perfumed room*. Then she summoned Helen, wishing to reunite the two lovers. Helen resisted – *shame it were to lie with that man* – but in vain; she had to obey the goddess. She went to join Paris, as besotted with love as ever. Was Aphrodite herself immune to the power of love? The threats she uses on Helen suggest she is not: *lest in rage / I give thee up, and loathe thee just as much / As I have loved thee wildly*. In Book XIV, the poet shows that even Zeus himself is powerless in the face of love.

The war might have ended there, since Menelaus has emerged victorious, but at the instigation of the gods a Trojan broke the truce and treacherously wounded Menelaus, which finally unleashed the battle. The only purpose of this episode is to show Helen and Paris, and the power of love.

LEFT
Hector and Menelaus fight for the body of Euphorbus, dish from Rhodes, 600 BC. Its profusion of decorative elements transforms a savage duel, described in Book XVII of *The Iliad*, into a perfectly balanced, timeless composition.

OPPOSITE
The Reconciliation of Paris and Helen, by Richard Westall (1765–1836). The Neoclassical style of the end of the 18th century struggles to capture the omnipotence of love and its goddess Aphrodite, as she watches over the reunion of the lovers.

As the sea-surge before the West wind's drive
Beats, wave on wave, upon the sounding shore –
First out at sea it gathers to a crest;
Then breaking on the beach it bellows loud,
But curving round the headland spouts aloft
And spews the salt froth high – so, rank on rank,
Now the battalions of the Danai moved
Without a pause, to war. Each captain gave
Command to his own troop; the others marched
With never a sound; a watcher would have thought
That great attendant host had not a voice
Among them, silent as they were for fear
Of their commanders; and on every man
Glittered the patterned mail in which he marched.
But for the Trojans – as inside the yard
Of some rich owner stand uncounted ewes
To yield their white milk, and they keep on bleating
To hear their young ones call – e'en so arose
A clamour down the whole wide Trojan host,
For not all of one voice and one tongue were they,
But mixed of speech, because they had been called
from many lands. And Ares urged them on,

The Feats
of the Warriors

Whereas grey-eyed Athene spurred the Greeks,
With Fear and Rout, and Strife who never flags,
Man-slaying Ares's sister and ally;
She that at first carries her crest low down,
But presently she plants her head in heaven,
Although her feet tread earth. And now she flung
Among them broadcast hatred as she passed
Amid the crowd, augmenting human woe.
Now when they had met and come to one same place,
There was a clash of shield and spear and rage
Of brazen-coated men; and bossy shields
Jarred each on each, and a great clang arose.
Then both were heard, the triumph and the wail
Of slain and slayers; and the earth ran blood.
As when two winter torrents racing down
The mountains to a meeting of the glens
Pour the strong waters of their mighty springs
Together in a deep ravine, and far
Among the hills the shepherd hears
The thunder of them; so were din and toil
Born as the battle joined.

Antilochus was the first to kill his man,
A Trojan warrior fully armoured who
Was active in the forefront, Echepolus,
Thalysius's son: he struck him on the peak
Of his hair-crested helmet and transfixed
His forehead, and the point went through the bone.
So darkness veiled his eyes, and down he fell,
As when a tower goes down in furious battle.
Now Elephenor prince, Chalcodon's son,
Chief of the proud Abantes, as he dropped
Caught at his feet to drag him out beyond
The range of shot, impatient all at once
To strip his armour off him; but his effort
Was shortly sped, for as he dragged the body,
Great-heart Agenor saw him: where the shield
Had left his side uncovered as he stooped,
He smote him, lunging with his bronze-tipped spear,
And loosed his limbs. So life deserted him:
But over his body followed bitter work
For Trojans and Achaeans: each at each
Like wolves they leapt, and grappled man with man.

Book IV, lines 422–472.

The First Clashes

THE FIRST DIRECT CONFRONTATION between the Achaeans and the Trojans was the first realisation of the announcement made in the Prologue. Death now enters the scene. After the general description, in which similes are frequently employed, the clashes begin between the 'soldiers of the front rank' (*promachoi*), and these take up the main part of the account. Some of these men achieve phenomenal feats of valour, which are described at length in the Books that follow: Diomedes, Agamemnon and Hector. The two kinds of description, collective combat and individual fights, are quite dissimilar. The former deals with clashes *en bloc*, between formations of warriors fighting shoulder to shoulder, advancing in a disciplined pattern, which for historians corresponds to the hoplite tactics of Greek warfare in Archaic and Classical times. The latter are personal duels, each man attacking or retreating on his own initiative in his quest for personal glory. The battle around the body of a front-rank fighter enables the poet to describe both types of combat together: the fate of the body, which is either desecrated by victorious enemies, stripped of its armour and left to the dogs and birds, or is recovered and honoured by allied forces, illustrates the distinction between a fine and glorious death and a hideous demise.

While the gods take sides, the poet mentions them in such a way as to make Ares, the god of war, and and his acolytes Fear, Rout and especially Strife the dominant figures on the battlefield. The image of the swelling wave recurs in the allegory of Strife, rising up from earth to heaven. From simile to allegory, the reality of war becomes ever more apparent as something pathetic rather than glorious: *multiplying human pain.*

Hoplite. One of the oldest examples (end of the 6th century BC) of a decoration painted on an earthenware plate, with the flesh in brown heightened with black line. The word KALOS (handsome) shows it was a lover's present.

Detail from a red-figured earthenware water jar dating from about 480 BC. The cuirass, the sword, the helmet and the shield stand out against a black background, devoid of any human presence.

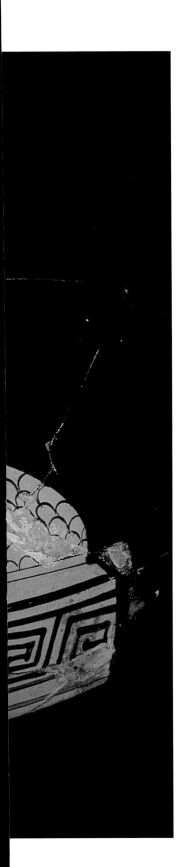

The point of view adopted for the first clash adds to this impression. It is one available only to the gods. We hear and see the battle as Zeus would have done, from afar and from high up, without distinguishing between the two camps. Everything is mixed together. Roars and cries of triumph, blows given and received (the Greek text succinctly says: 'Men who kill, men who die') make just one *great clang* and one river of blood. The simile which follows increases the effect of movement, the action almost accelerating as it moves from the *mighty springs* of the mountain torrents to the *din* of battle. There is a kind of pathetic objectivity which is characteristic of Homer's art.

It is also particularly effective in the descriptions of individual deaths. The hand-to-hand duels, which occupy the last part of Book IV, all lead to the same end. Heroic battles almost never feature non-fatal wounds, and death is always prompt. Either a warrior escapes the blow or he dies from it. The first deaths in *The Iliad* are almost all of unknown soldiers who only exist in order to be killed. The poet and his audiences were much more passionate about death, and the way it snatches life away, than about the combat itself, which is not often described in detail. The weapon, the way it penetrates the body, seen in close-up, is dreadful enough, sometimes almost unbearably so, as in this much later fight:

...the spear of bronze went through
Below the brain and shattered the white bones,
Dashed out his teeth, and filled his eyes with blood;
And blood he spurted gaping through his mouth
And nose; and death's dark cloud encompassed him.

Book XVI, lines 345–350.

Diomedes Wounds Ares

Diomedes is the star of Book V, achieving the most extraordinary feats. With the help of the goddess Athene, who accompanies him throughout, he even goes so far as to wound two divinities, first Aphrodite, goddess of love, then Ares, god of war; only wounding them, of course, because you cannot kill an immortal. Ares and Aphrodite, who are lovers in *The Odyssey*, are here brother and sister. Love and war were closely bound to Troy from the beginning, and it is not without significance that the two divinities to be wounded by a human are patrons of the city. Also that no one complains about this, except them.

The gods in combat (Attic pelike or storage jar, detail), painted in a lively style at the end of the 5th century BC and the beginning of the 4th.

The detail shows Poseidon and Ares fighting the Giants during the war that asserted the supremacy of Zeus and the Olympians.

But as soon as Ares, bane of mortals, saw
Good Diomedes, he left huge Periphas
To lie there on the spot where he had killed him
And taken his life away; and straight he made
For knightly Diomedes. And when they
Were come in touch, each moving towards the other,
First Ares over yoke and reins took aim
With his bronze spear, in his fierce hope to have
Tydides's life; but grey-eyed Pallas caught it
And sent it rushing idly o'er the car.
In turn Tydides good at need let drive
With spear of bronze at Ares, and Athene
Sent it right home against his groin, where he
Was girded with a kilt: he struck him there
And pierced and mangled his fair flesh, and plucked
The weapon out. Then brazen Ares roared
As loud as nine, nay, as ten thousand men
Send up a war-shout when the battle joins;
And shivering seized the Trojans and Achaeans
For fear, so loud insatiate Ares roared.

Book V, lines 846–863.

The poet makes a contrast between the two wounds. Aphrodite receives a simple graze, just enough to make her leave the field of battle. She shed only a little blood, or rather:

… ichor, such
As fills the veins of blessed gods, for they
Neither eat bread nor drink the beaded wine,
And so are bloodless and are named immortals.

Book V, lines 340–342.

It is an apt moment to note the insurmountable difference between men and gods. When Alexander the Great was wounded he, according to Plutarch, remembered these lines of Homer: 'What flows here, my friends, is blood and not ichor such as is shed by the blessed gods.' Aphrodite runs to take refuge with her mother, Dione (Homer does not use the horrible genealogy devised by Hesiod), in Olympus, protesting and weeping. Zeus, her father, advises her to attend to her own affairs, the *lovely works of wedlock*, and not to war.

On the other hand, at the end of the Book, when Ares sped up to heaven, the wound in his groin was serious. A mortal being would have died immediately from it. Ares himself was only saved by Zeus calling for the gods' physician to treat him urgently. Ares had directed the Trojan counter-attack, but the terror aroused by his cries went well beyond his own camp: both his Trojan allies and their Achaean adversaries trembled with fear. When, like Aphrodite, he went to complain to his father about his misfortune, Homer stresses the isolation of this *scourge of the world* amongst the gods themselves. Zeus scolded him, seeing in him *the hard tough temper* of his mother Hera:

I execrate thee most of all the gods
Who hold Olympus; wars and fights and frays
Are all thou ever carest for.

Book V, lines 890–891.

War itself seems to be condemned in the blow that struck Ares.

This wound gave the Achaeans such an advantage that Hector returned to Troy to beseech the gods. As he was returning to the fight, he met his wife Andromache and their son Astyanax. She implored him in vain to think of them and remain in Troy.

Then said great Hector of the flashing helm:
'Yes, and I think of all these things, my wife;
But feel a fearful shame before the Trojans
And Trojan women with their trailing robes,
If like a coward I evade the war.
And mine own heart forbids it: I have learned
To be a brave man always and to fight
Among the Trojan front accomplishing
My father's lofty honour and mine own.
For well I know it in my heart and soul,
Shall come a day when sacred Ilios
Will be laid low, and Priam, and the folk
Of Priam, lord of the good ashwood spear.
But not my sorrow for the Trojans' trouble
And Hecuba herself and Priam king
And all my brothers – that brave company
Who shall go down in dust beneath the hands
Of foes – so moves me as thy suffering doth
When some bronze-clad Achaean leads thee off
Weeping, and takes the day of freedom from thee.
And there, maybe in Argos, shalt thou weave
At some strange woman's bidding, or bear water
From Hyperia or Messeis's stream,
Harshly abused, with strong constraint upon thee.
And one who sees thee weep perchance will say:
"That is the wife of Hector, who was best
In fight of all the knightly sons of Troy,
When men did battle around Ilios."
So one may say, and unto thee will be
Sorrow renewed, for lack of one like me
To keep away the day of bondage; only
Let me be dead, with earth heaped on me, ere
I hear thy crying as they drag thee off!'
So glorious Hector said, and stretched his arms
To take his son: but the child cried and huddled
Close to the breast of his neat-girdled nurse,
Feared at his father's looks, scared by the bronze
And plume of horse's hair ...

Book VI, lines 440–471.

The Exploits of Hector

The Farewells of Hector and Andromache,
by Angelika Kauffmann (1741–1807).
Thanks to the chiaroscuro, this
Neoclassical canvas is interpreted
with sensitivity and, some would
say, sentimentality.

The Farewell to Andromache

THE DEPARTURE OF THE FULLY ARMED WARRIOR, and the farewell to his weeping family, was a scene often represented in Greek ceramics, and was certainly a sad experience common in daily life, such was the frequency of wars in those times. This departure is justified by the ideals and the duty to be courageous to which Hector brings a new definition: *To be a brave man always and to fight / Among the Trojan front accomplishing / My father's lofty honour and mine own.* These lines summarise the ideals of aristocratic rivalry, and the 'agonal' ideal which characterises Greek civilisation and which Henri-Irénée Marrou likens to the knightly ideal in his *History of Education in Antiquity.* The prospect of Troy's defeat and fall cannot stop Hector. This prospect exists, however, and is even presented as an absolute certainty.

Troy is destined to perish: everyone knows it, such is the history of Troy, and it is not within the poet's powers to modify this legendary fact. Priam will die, and all the men too, and the women will be taken into slavery, as we see in *The Trojan Women* and *Hecuba* by Euripides. Astyanax will be assassinated, to ensure he never avenges the death of his father. It is a feature of Homer's genius that he transforms this need for narrative order into a terrible presentiment, even a personal certainty on the part of Hector: *For well I know it in my heart and soul.* His certainty does not, however, go so far as to envisage the supreme misfortune, the death of his son, and the reader who knows the fate of Astyanax feels the pathetic power of this omission. The worst that Hector can foresee is Andromache being taken into slavery. As a couple, Hector and Andromache are the opposite of Paris and Helen. They are highly modest and tender. Andromache is given these extraordinary lines as she tries to persuade Hector not to fight:

Hector, thou to me
Art father, mother, brother, as thou art
My husband full of life.

Book VI, lines 429–430.

For her, their conjugal relations absorb all the other family relationships. Hector acknowledges this privilege: the idea that his wife might be taken into slavery, and the premonition of his own fate, are worse for him than the death of his father, his mother and brothers. The hero even imagines what might be said in front of

Andromache when she is a slave, far from Troy and her past glory. What the poet primarily describes as Hector's own anguish is thus enlarged into a compassionate reaction that all men can share.

For a moment, Hector takes off his helmet, to embrace his son. He asks the gods that Astyanax might surpass him in glory – which the gods do not allow – then gives the child back to Andromache, sending her back to her women's work while the men go off to war: *She took him to her fragrant breast / Smiling through tears.*

Hector against Ajax

Hector did not set off to battle alone: his brother Paris, *Glowing in armour like the sun afire*, accompanied him. Instead of resuming combat, the rival armies were persuaded by the gods to organise a second duel, this time setting Hector, the best of the Trojans, against the best of the Achaeans after Achilles, Ajax, *giant Ajax, bulwark of the Achaeans*, who was appointed after lots were drawn. The two heroes fought for a whole day without either seizing victory. When night fell, their companions separated them. Hector and Ajax marked their fine struggle by exchanging precious gifts: Hector gave Ajax the sword with which, much later, after the death of Achilles, he would kill himself. This exchanging of presents after a day of bloody combat may seem surprising. But in *The Iliad*, opponents respected their foes as much as they hated each other, so much so that they could even break off the fight as more or less friends. *That men may say, Trojans and Greeks alike, / 'See, out of soul-consuming rivalry / They fought, and parted in a pact of friendship.'* Both camps spoke Greek. The distinction between Greeks and Barbarians did not yet exist; it would only appear with the Median Wars between Persia and Greece at the end of the Archaic period, and it was later still, with Euripides and Isocrates, that the Trojan War was reinterpreted as the first offensive of the united Greeks against the Barbarians, preparing the way, as it were, for the conquests of Alexander. Even the notion of Greece did not exist at the time.

Rather than allowing the duel to continue, the leaders agreed a truce so that each camp could honour its dead by burning their bodies. *Hard task it was to recognise each man.* In each camp, the bodies were washed, piled on the pyres which, in silence, were lit, so that the souls of the dead could go to the sacred underworld. The Achaeans also built a rampart to protect their ships from an attack by the Trojans.

Ajax by Pietro de Muttoni (1605–1678).

So with high hearts they sat all through the night
Along the no-man's land: and their camp fires
Were burning thickly. And as when in heaven
About the shining moon the stars appear
Surpassing bright, and all the air is still,
And every peak and headland high and vale
Stands out, and from the firmament breaks open
The infinity of air; and all the stars
Are seen, and joy is in the shepherd's heart:
So multitudinous between the ships
Ans Xanthus's streams appeared the bivouac fires
The Trojans burned in front of Ilios.
A thousand fires were burning on the plain,
And by the side of each sat fifty men
In the hot fire light; and their horses stood
Munching their meal of spelt and barley white,
Beside the cars, awaiting fair-throned Dawn.

Book VIII, lines 550–565.

The Trojans Scent Victory

The Mission

ZEUS, RESOLVING TO CARRY OUT THE PROMISE HE HAD MADE TO THETIS, then forbade the gods to take part in combat between men and retired, *exulting in his glory*, to Mount Ida, from where he could see both the *town of Troy and the Achaean ships*. A second day of fighting began, in the course of which the Achaeans suffered a serious defeat. That evening, the Trojans had established themselves on the plain. The camp fires echoed the fire of the stars. The comparison between the Trojan camp and the starry sky is particularly effective because it is more than a comparison. In the night, we look from the camp of men up to the immensity of the heavens, as the stars break through the clouds. The situation was so serious for the Achaeans that they tried to win over Achilles with a solemn mission, authorised by Agamemnon and led by the fiery Diomedes, old Nestor, the eloquent Odysseus and Phoenix, Achilles' tutor. The whole of Book IX is devoted to these various discussions. But Achilles did not accept the sumptuous presents offered to him, and shut himself away in his anger, despite the warning of Phoenix who, in an allegory, described the Delusion attached to the steps of someone who refuses to be soothed by the Prayers. From then on, Achilles was to pursue the path of misfortune.

> 'Tis so; for Prayers
> Are daughters of high Zeus. They have a squint;
> They hobble; they are wrinkled; yet they do
> Their office, plodding on the trail of Sin;
> But Sin is strong and fleet of foot and so
> Runs far ahead of all the Prayers, and goes
> Before them over the whole world and makes
> Men stumble; but the Prayers come after her
> And heal the hurt. Whoso regards the maids
> Of Zeus when they draw near, him they reward
> Abundantly and hear him when he prays;
> But if a man denies them, if he is stubborn
> And puts them from him, then they go and beg
> Zeus, son of Cronos, to let Ate come
> To bring him down and make him pay the price.

Book IX, lines 502–512.

PREVIOUS PAGE
Zeus, encouraged by Cupids (lower right), takes the hand of his wife Hera, who is pushed by a winged spirit (symbolising Mount Ida?) and separated from him by a votive column.

ABOVE
Old Nestor, king of Pylos, who plays host to Telemachus in *The Odyssey*, is the prototype of wisdom. Detail from an Attic vase of the 5th century BC.

The Trojans Scent Victory   59

Agamemnon Strikes

After a strange night attack described in Book X, Books XI to XVIII show both the realisation of Zeus's plan, in other words the continuing failure of the Achaeans so long as Achilles stays out of the fight, and the threats which are heaped upon Achilles himself. Further events include manoeuvres by deities on the side of the Achaeans. First of all King Agamemnon, having tried to effect a reconciliation with Achilles, is now allowed his moment of superiority as he drives the Trojans back to their city walls.

> Like cattle scattered by a lion coming
> By dead of night upon them. All are scattered,
> But one sees death right on her: first he takes
> And breaks her neck in his strong teeth and then
> He gorges on the blood and all the guts.
> So Agamemnon, son of Atreus, hunted
> The Trojans …
>
> Book XI, lines 172–177.

But Zeus tells Hector that once Agamemnon is wounded, the Trojans will win back the advantage, and keep it until that evening. The promise is realised, and the Achaeans retreat as far as the rampart built to protect their ships, which Hector finally breaches after three attacks have been repelled. Only the secret intervention of the god Poseidon prevents the ships from being set on fire.

Hera's Trickery

Hera too wanted to save the Achaeans and decided to distract Zeus from the fight by arousing his desire. This interlude, which was to arouse the indignation of several philosophers, Plato in particular, at Homer's offhand and, to them, scandalous way of representing the gods, connects with the theme concerning the origins of the war: the power of love, which even conquers the king of the gods himself.

Hera in chiton and coat, wearing a diadem and carrying a sceptre (detail from an Attic bowl with a white background painted c. 470 BC). This Hera in majesty conveys the formidable power of the deity, who was the patroness of the city of Argos.

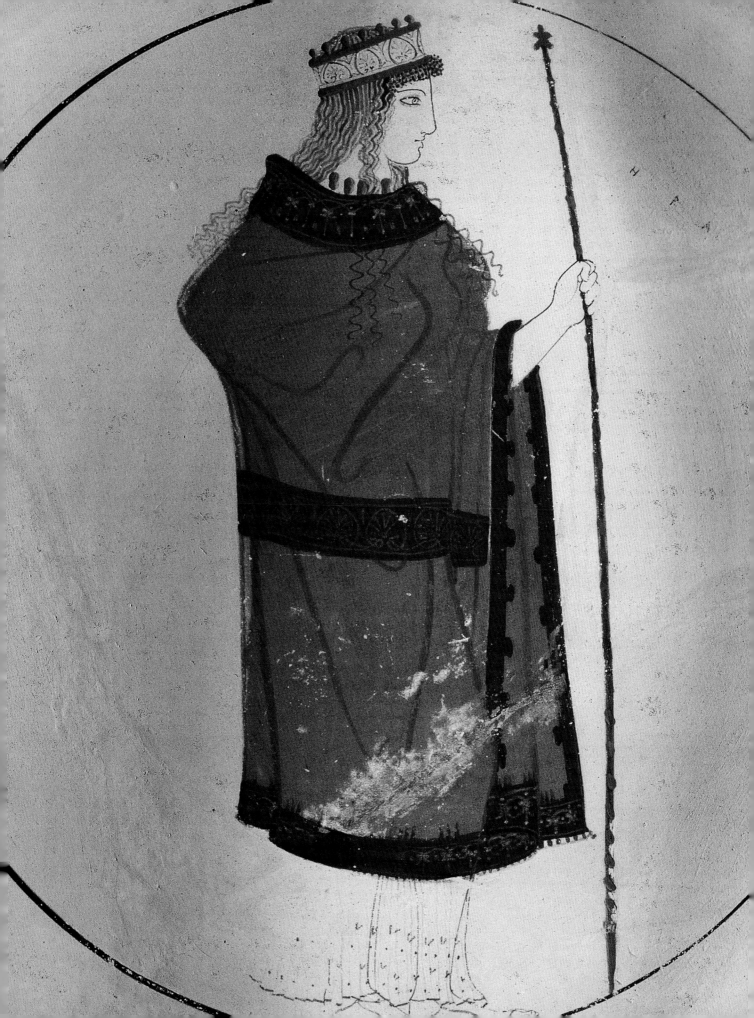

Jupiter and Juno on Mount Ida, by James Barry (1741–1806). In *The Iliad*, at least, it is not the goddess's splendid breasts which attract Zeus, but a more complicated combination of amorous rhetoric, magical robes and seductive finery. The painter (who uses the gods' Latin names) has nonetheless captured the ardour of the king of the gods very well.

Then cunningly Queen Hera answered him:
'Majestic Cronides, what hast thou said!
If thou art eager now to lie with me
On Ida's peaks, where all is plain to view,
How would it be if we were seen asleep
By some one of the gods who live for ever,
Who went and told the tale to all the gods?
Not I could bear to rise from bed and go
Back to thy house; 'twould be a shameful thing.
But if thou wilt, if this is thy good pleasure,
Thou hast a chamber which thy son Hephaestus
Constructed for thee, and upon the posts
He hung close-fitting doors; there let us go
And lay us down, since bed is thy desire.'
But Zeus who rules the clouds replied to her:
'Ah, Hera, never fear that god or man
Shall see; so will I veil thee in a cloud,
A cloud of gold, through which not Helios even
Should watch us two, although there is not light
So keen as his for seeing.'
So said Cronion, and he caught his wife
Into his arms: beneath them earth divine
Made fresh new grass to grow, and dewy lotus
And crocus and thick tender hyacinth
That raised them from the ground. Therein they lay,
Wrapped in a beautiful and golden mist
Whence rainbow dew-drops fell.
So then on Gargarus's peak the Father slept
Serenely, overcome by sleep and love,
His arms around his wife.

Book XIV, lines 329–353.

The special point about this episode is the way Homer describes with technical precision the deceitful (diabolical would be the Christian way of putting it) manner in which Hera arouses her husband's desire while pretending to be a modest woman. Given the way Homer describes the usual, somewhat tense relationship between Zeus and Hera, the success of her plan does not initially seem to be guaranteed.

The seduction process begins with a modest description of Hera washing and anointing herself. Then she dresses, with particular attention paid to her robe, brooches and belt; the veil which covers her head (Greek women wore veils) is *bright as the sun*. Her next step is to visit Aphrodite, who specialises in love. Hera does not tell her the truth. She asks the goddess for a magic charm that she can give, she claims, to her old adopted parents who are continually quarrelling, and so *set them in each other's arms again*. This projection of her own relations with Zeus, and of the plan she has in mind, onto her parents is a real stroke of the poet's imagination. Aphrodite obeys, but Homer clearly lets it be known that she is not deceived. She gives Hera the golden band ...

> ... with every kind of charm
> Wrought into it; there is love in it and passion
> And amorous talk, that tempter who can steal
> The wisdom of the wise.

Book XIV, lines 215–217.

As a final precaution, Hera goes to see the god Sleep, asking him to send Zeus to sleep after they have made love. This is a rather delicate business, because Sleep has a bitter memory of the last time he performed this service for Hera. But Herea promises him the love of the beautiful Pasitheë, whom he had desired for a long time, and Sleep agrees. So equipped, Hera approaches Zeus on the summit of Mount Ida. The plan succeeds perfectly, but the treacherous Hera excites great Zeus still further by telling him too that she wants to visit her parents and reconcile them, and that she has just come to see him, as a submissive wife, to ask his permission to go. Zeus almost interrupts her:

Zeus who rules the clouds
Saw her, and when he saw her, all at once
Love mantled his wise heart, as when at first
They went and shared the bed of love together
Without their parents' knowledge [...]
For journeying there another day will do:
Now let us to bed and take delight in love.
For never, Hera, hath such flood of love
For goddess or for woman overwhelmed
The heart within me ...

Book XIV, lines 293–296 and 313–316.

Very Human Gods

We know of course that the gods are immortal and have their own special food, nectar and ambrosia, as well as special body fluid which, for want of a better word, the poet calls 'ichor', after the name for human serous fluids, as opposed to blood, which was mentioned in the episode of Aphrodite being wounded. They thus have a permanence that humans lack. Material contingencies are less important to them than they are to humans: they can move easily from one side of the world to the other, using their magic powers at will to transform the environment, remotely control the flight of weapons and carry their favourites about. This gives the poet a freedom of action that he uses liberally. But the gods in *The Iliad* are, as we see, very human too: there are Zeus and Hera acting like young lovers in a hurry, but discreet as well, Zeus the male proud of his conquests and oblivious of the effect that enumerating them might have, Hera playing the seductress and lying outright to fool her aged husband – this might all seem inappropriate to the notion of divinity. Philosophers and Christians would emphatically agree with this. But people will still read Homer regardless. For while the epic action constantly unfolds on two levels, the divine and the human, each seems equally easy, or difficult, to understand.

The Turning-point in the Fighting

When Zeus awoke, everything was very different. He saw Hector wounded and the Trojans in flight. He was furious and quickly restored order both in Olympus and on the battlefield, from which he banished Poseidon. He revealed the future to Hera: Patroclus would return to the fray, Hector would kill him, then Achilles would kill Hector, and finally the Achaeans would capture Troy. The epic obeys what Tzvetan Todorov has called an 'intrigue of predestination', in which the interest is in the way fate makes itself apparent, and in the way we look forward to the outcome rather than in the outcome itself. The deeds accomplished by Hector from this point onward led the Trojans as far as the Greek ships. Despite Ajax's heroic defence, one of them caught fire. Then Patroclus, Achilles' most faithful friend, followed up a suggestion made to him by old Nestor in Book XI, and obtained permission from Achilles to fight, but only to rescue the Achaeans and then to stop before he reached the ramparts of Troy: *Nor, out of sheer delight in war and fray / And Trojan-killing, lead thy troops to Troy [...] / ...turn back, once thou has shown the ship / A beacon-light, and leave the others there / Across the plain to battle*. If he disobeyed, Achilles predicted that he was likely to be caught by the god Apollo. Patroclus put on Achilles' armour and went to the head of his contingent, the Myrmidons.

They charged the Trojans. Out they poured apace
Like wasps beside the road, whom boys, being boys,
Provoke by constantly annoying them
There in their wayside nests, and, silly children,
Cause indiscriminate hurt to many people.

Book XVI, lines 258–262.

The effect was immediate: the Trojans withdrew to the walls of Troy. Several Trojan heroes were killed, in particular Sarpedon, although he was a son of Zeus, and the driver of Hector's chariot, Cebriones, around whom a bloody fight took place, then *Down from the well-made car he plunged, and life / Quitted his bones*. But Patroclus, excited by the fury of the fighting, did not obey the orders that Achilles had so clearly given him.

But Hector, when he saw great-heart Patroclus
Retiring wounded by the pointed bronze,
Came near him through the ranks, and plunged a spear
Into his groin, and ran the head clean through.
Thundering he fell, and on the Achaean host
Brought huge dismay. And as a lion in fight
O'ercomes a strenuous boar, when both of them
Fight in their pride upon the mountain peaks
Over a scanty water whereat both
Are bent on drinking, and the panting boar
Is mastered by the lion in his strength;
So from Menoetius's valiant son, when he
Had slaughtered many, Hector, Priam's son,
Took life away, with a close thrust of spear.
And boasting over him spoke winged words:
'Patroclus, thou didst think to sack my city,
And rob the Trojan dames of freedom's day,
And bear them off in ships to thine own land.

The Death of Patroclus

Fool! for in front of him the galloping steeds
Of Hector strain to war, and I myself
Am the best spear among the fighting Trojans
To keep from them the day of servitude.
But thee, the vultures shall devour thee here,
O luckless man! Achilles in his valour
Avails thee not, who, when thou camest and he
Remained behind, must have adjured thee straitly:
"Come not, Patroclus, master of the horse,
Back to the hollow ships, I bid thee, till
Thou gash the bloody tunic on the breast
Of man-destroying Hector." So, for sure, said he,
And he beguiled thee in thy foolishness.'
Then feebly, knight Patroclus, didst thou say:
'Now boast thy biggest, Hector, for to thee
Have Zeus Cronion and Apollo given
The triumph, and have slain me without effort,
For they it was who took my armour from me.
But if a score of men like thee had met me,
Here should they all have perished by my spear.
No! deadly Fate and Leto's son have killed me,
And then, of men, Euphorbus; in my slaying

Thou art but third. And one thing more have I
To say, and do thou lay it to thy heart.
I say thou hast not long to live thyself
But death and potent fate stand close beside thee,
And thou art doomed to be subdued before
Achilles, matchless son of Aeacus.'
The end of death enclosed him as he spoke.

Book XVI, lines 818–842.

Attic bowl painted in the 'severe'
style at the end of the Archaic
period, showing the Fall of Troy
as described in a lost epic, *The
Ilioupersis*. In one notable element,
lower left, Andromache holding
a club vainly tries to protect her
son Astyanax.

A Sad Omen

BOOK XVI includes more comparisons with animal fights than any other: a lion killing a bull, two lions fighting over a doe, then, as here, a lion fiercely attacking a powerful wild boar. Such scenes certainly did not occur in everyday life, even if we allow that there were still lions in Greece in Homer's time, which had been represented in art since Mycenaean times and appeared on the coins of some classical cities; they were, however, images familiar to the poem's audiences. By placing this fight *upon the mountain peaks*, Homer isolates and distances it, like a work of art, just before returning to a close-up of the lance which pierces the body of Patroclus. Hector, in a sense, only finished off Patroclus, who had already been deprived of all protection by Apollo and then was wounded by Euphorbus. In some respects, therefore, the comparison is inapt. But that *scanty water* at which *both / Are bent on drinking*, may also represent the short time left to each of them before they die. In the sense that the lesson of the duel is that death awaits both men, the image is perfectly correct. The death of Patroclus in effect announces the death of Hector, which in turn will announce the death of Achilles. This is a clear example of the deliberative character of *The Iliad*'s composition.

Poor Fools

In epic duels, insults often precede the fight, forming an initial, oratory phase of the struggle. This is not so here, because the fight is unequal, and above all because the words exchanged have a significance which surpasses that of the duel itself. We can see here a recurring feature, the contrast between the illusion which seizes the triumphant warrior, carried away by that mad ardour we have already encountered, and the clarity of the dying man. *Fool!* cries Hector, along with other similar insults, but while Patroclus has also been carried away before by delusion and folly, here it is Hector who does not know what he is saying. Moreover, Achilles never actually spoke the words Hector attributes to him, and in fact had warned Patroclus not to become heavily involved in the battle. In Book VI, when he said goodbye to Andromache, Hector was terrifyingly lucid; now he is portrayed as blind. It is typical of Homer's art to present the same hero being both clear and blind to the truth,

OPPOSITE
Achilles tends the wounded Patroclus (red-figured bowl from Sosias dated c. 500 BC). This famous bowl in the 'severe' style features a competely harmonious portrait of the two friends, seemingly bound together by the bandage which Achilles is applying. Even though their eyes (which from now on were represented in profile) do not meet, we clearly sense the pain of Patroclus and the rapt attention of Achilles. The scene shows an episode that does not appear in *The Iliad*.

while readers will feel the inexorable character of the announcement of his death, conveyed to him by a dying man.

The heroes themselves are thus no more than *poor fools*. The Greek word used here, and in other rude remarks uttered by the heroes, and which Achilles later levels at Hector, literally means 'Child incapable of speech'. In a myth in his epic poem *Works and Days*, which tells the story of the human peoples and human decadence from the golden people to the iron people, Hesiod begins by comparing the golden people, who are happy, to the silver people, who are already guilty. The men of silver indulge in excess (*hubris*), and no longer respect either the gods or justice. But the characteristic trait of this people is that the men of silver, before they become adults and commit their crimes, spend *a hundred years* as *big children*, as *poor fools*. In *The Iliad*, it is the adult male who remains an eternal child in relation to the future which he is ignorant of, deliberately or otherwise, and the power of the gods. He is incapable of speaking and thinking, but at the same time thinks he is all-powerful.

Book XVII is entirely devoted to the fighting around the body of Patroclus. Menelaus, a lion 'gorging on blood', kills Euphorbus then, like a lion chased away by dogs and shepherds, he retreats from Hector but, with the help of Ajax, *like a lion o'er his whelps*, returns to the attack to take Achilles' personal armour back to him, along with the body of his friend. Attacks and counter-attacks ensue.

The earth grew wet with purple blood,
And of the Trojans and their strong allies
The dead fell thick and fast.

Book XVII, lines 360–361.

Hector snatches the armour of Achilles, but the two Ajaxes manage to remove Patroclus's body from the Trojans, holding off their attacks like *some wooded ridge that lies / Athwart a plain, and holds the water back*, while Nestor's young son Antilochus goes to tell Achilles the terrible news.

The Return of Achilles and the Death of Hector

ACHILLES RETURNS TO THE FIGHTING TO AVENGE PATROCLUS BY KILLING HECTOR, BUT HE KNOWS THAT HE TOO MUST DIE. SUCH IS THE MISFORTUNE OF MEN. AND MEN HAVE ONLY ONE WAY OF SOFTENING THE BLOW: THROUGH THEIR GRIEF.

The gods have wrought affliction for my soul, / Such as my mother once declared to me. / The best man of the Myrmidons, she said, / While I still lived, should by the Trojans' hands / Forsake the sunlight.

While thus he pondered in his mind and heart,
The son of lordly Nestor came beside him,
Shedding hot tears, and spoke the grievous news:
'Alas! brave Peleus's son, that thou must hear
Most bitter news – would that it were not so!
Fallen Patroclus lies, and over his body
They fight – and it is naked, for the arms
Bright-crested Hector hath.'
He spoke, and a black cloud of grief enwrapped
Achilles, and with both his hands he took
The sooty dust and poured it o'er his head
And fouled his gracious face; black hung the ash
About his fragrant tunic: in the dust
Himself he stretched him, great and greatly fallen,
And with his fingers tore and marred his hair.
The women slaves whom both had taken as spoil,
Achilles and Patroclus, shrieked aloud
For grief of heart: out from the door they ran
About the brave Achilles, and they all
Beat on their breasts, and each one's limbs were loosed.
And on the other side Antilochus
Wept and bewailed, holding Achilles' hands
As that great heart lamented, for he feared
That he might take the steel and cut his throat.
So terribly Achilles made his moan.

Book XVIII, lines 15–34.

The Grief of Achilles

The Greek Heroes Weep

THE FLIGHT OF THE ACHAEANS OVER THE PLAIN had aroused a feeling of impending disaster in Achilles, which Antilochus only confirmed, *The son of lordly Nestor came beside him, / Shedding hot tears.* Heroes in *The Iliad* and *The Odyssey* weep like heroines. They never do so in battle, even in the most fearsome engagements, or when wounded or faced with death, but in moments of reflection, reunion and grief. Virile modesty in the face of tears would come later.

Achilles immediately performs the ritual gestures of grief: covering himself with ashes, tearing his hair. His entourage do the same: there are cries of grief and breast-beating. The line *in the dust / Himself he stretched him,* which in Greek contains poetic effects that are almost untranslatable, was partly used in Book XVI, to describe the dead Cebriones. It is also repeated at the end of *The Odyssey*: *but you lay, / Great, fallen greatly, in the eddying dust, / Your feats of knighthood vanished quite away.* However, in this passage, the lines are addressed to the dead Achilles in the underworld. The words were perhaps borrowed from epics which told of the death of Achilles; whether this is so or not, the grief of Achilles foreshadows his death to come. Antilochus is nevertheless afraid he will kill himself. Achilles does not take his own life, but by resuming the fight his death is implied. This is confirmed by his mother, Thetis, much moved by her son's cries, whose echo Homer describes as travelling as far as her palace in the depths of the sea.

But weeping Thetis answered him again:
'Short-lived wilt thou be then, my child, by what
Thou sayst; for after Hector has been killed
Thy death is close at hand.'
Then deeply moved swift-foot Achilles said:
'O let me die at once, for that I was not
To help my comrade in his hour of need!'

Book XVIII, lines 94–99.

In rage against
The Trojans he did on the heavenly gifts
Which by his toil Hephaestus made for him.
And first about his legs he girt the greaves,
Shapely and held by silver ankle-clips,
And then put on the corslet round his chest:
About his neck he threw the sword of bronze
With silver studs, and last he took the shield,
That great stiff shield from which there went afar
A brightness like the moon's. And e'en as when
Across the sea appears a beacon fire
To sailors; and it burns high up the hills
In some lone farm; but sore against their will
The storm-winds bear them o'er the fishy deep
Far from their friends; so from Achilles' shield
Fair and ornate, the splendour went to heaven.
Then he picked up and set upon his head
The heavy helmet; like a star it shone,
That helm of horse-hair crest, with plumes of gold
Waving about it which Hephaestus set
Thick round the peak. Then great Achilles made
Proof of himself in armour, to be sure
It fitted him and gave his bright limbs play;
And it became as though it were wings to him
And bore aloft the shepherd of the people.

Book XIX, lines 364–386.

The Fury of Achilles

PREVIOUS PAGE
Thetis in Hephaestus's forge (Pompeian
fresco, AD 50).

ABOVE
The theme of Vulcan's forge (the Latin
name for Hephaestus) has often been
taken up by painters. It stresses the
skills of military craftsmen, and allows
painters and the figurative arts to
outdo the feats of poetry. Flemish
School, 16th century.

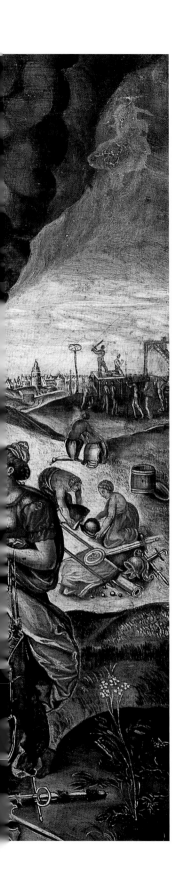

A Warrior's Fury

THETIS GAVE IN TO THE WILL OF HER SON, and even went to fetch new arms that the blacksmith god Hephaestus had undertaken to forge specially for him. Without waiting for these, Achilles moved on to the plain, and only needed to shout his war cry three times to set the Trojans fleeing and ensure forever the body of Patroclus, which he now finally saw, dead. On the Trojan side, it was Hector who was blinded by a warlike fury and ignored the advice of his companions. He would fight Achilles: '*And know to which of us the Olympian will / Award the boast.*'

At the beginning of Book XIX, Achilles received new arms from his mother, and then prepared himself for battle, after a reconciliation scene with Agamemnon, which put an end to Achilles' anger, but replaced it with his fury with the Trojans and Hector. Zeus's plan was thus realised: the honour of Achilles was re-established, but in a way that would multiply the number of deaths and bring Achilles closer to death.

The Arms of Achilles

In epics, a warrior setting out for battle always arms himself in the same way, and the same words are often used to describe this 'typical scene'. The shin protectors, or greaves, are made of leather but sometimes, as here, are covered with bronze plates, and ankle guards are fastened to them. The cuirass, as worn by leading warriors, is dressed with metal. Then the hero takes his sword, which he hangs from a sling worn over the right shoulder, and his shield, made from multiple layers of skin adorned with bronze. Finally he puts on his plumed helmet. Now he is ready to take his spear and mount the chariot and let its driver take him onto the field of battle. This is how warfare was conducted in what the historians call the Bronze Age – even though the poem makes several references to iron – and the 'bronze people' described by Hesiod in his famous story, a people who think only *of the wailing works of Ares and excessive deeds.*

The Shield

Homer has already given similar accounts of Paris arming himself in Book III, of Agamemnon in Book XI, Patroclus in book XVI and Hector in Book XVII. But there is a gradual progression from one scene to the next, a build-up from the beautiful warrior to the king of kings, then to two heroes who wear Achilles' first set of arms, and finally to Achilles himself. These scenes portray a kind of heraldic celebration of courage and heroic valour.

The divine arms that Hephaestus made for Achilles are exceptional. A hundred and twenty lines are devoted to the shield, with its admirable motifs which form a universe of their own: all the stars are shown there, and *two fine cities of men*, one at peace, the other at war, and a great ploughed field, and regal harvests, the grapes being picked to the sound of the lute, and herds of oxen, and finally, to crown everything, an image of a Minoan dancing floor.

This first description of an objet d'art in Western literature (made by the process traditionally known as *ekphrasis*) transports the reader briefly into an atmosphere of feasting and luxury, of youthfulness and life. The poetry rivals figurative art in the way it suggests the movements of the dance, the pirouettes of the acrobats. The scene with the shield provides *The Iliad* with a calming counterpoint, and a *mise en abyme* of the transformation into a work of art, through poetry, of the joys and misfortunes of men.

> Now first of all he made a great stiff shield,
> Adorning every part of it
> A brilliant flashing rim, three-fold, to which
> Was linked a silver belt. Five layers made up
> The shield itself, and on its face he worked
> With craftsman skill much curious device. [...]
> And on it too the famous cripple shaped
> A dancing-floor, like that in Knossos wide

Which Daedalus for fair-haired Ariadne
Once built. And lads and lasses dearly-wooed
Danced with their hands on one another's wrists.
The girls wore soft fine linen, and the lads
Close-woven tunics lightly glossed with oil.
The girls had pretty garlands, and the lads
Had golden dirks, on silver sword-slings hung.
And now with practised feet as light they ran
As when a potter sits and tries the wheel
That fits his hands, to see if it runs true;
And now in line they swayed towards one another;
And round the lovely dance there stood a crowd
Close-packed, enjoying it; and in the midst
To lead the dance a pair of acrobats
Went whirling by them.

Book XVIII, lines 478–482, 590–606.

Scenes fairly similar to those portrayed on Achilles' shield do in fact appear on Cretan frescoes in Knossos; these were discovered at the beginning of the 20th century, and too freely restored by Arthur Evans. Archaeologists also found dance halls, with terraces for the spectators. The spectacular discoveries made in the island of Thera from 1967, such as the miniature fresco called 'Of the Boats', provided another landmark. Much later, a prince's house or a funeral building, it is uncertain which, was discovered at Lefkandi, in Euboeia in 1981. This was from the beginning of the period known as the 'Dark Age', around 1000, and revealed a series of bronze vases with figurative ornamentation (fighting and hunting scenes) which also established a continuity with the earlier Mycenaean period and indicated, like other more recent tombs, the existence of commercial contacts and the handing down of valuable objects among members of the aristocracy. It may have been in the context of such bequests that the poet was able to find the source of his inspiration.

FOLLOWING PAGES
Achilles Setting Off to Avenge the Death of Patroclus, by Théodore Géricault (1791–1824).

Achilles and the Horse Xanthos

Just when they are about to set off, Xanthos, one of the horses pulling Achilles'
chariot, actually speaks, something quite exceptional in epics, and warns Achilles
of his impending death, to which he replies angrily in a tone which is to
dominate the rest of the story:

> 'Why, Xanthos, dost thou prophesy my death?
> 'Tis not thy office. Well I know myself
> That here it is appointed me to perish
> Far from my mother and my father dear;
> But all the same I will not cease, till I
> Have driven the Trojans to disgust of war.'

Book XIX, lines 420–423.

Book XX describes how Achilles furiously attacks the Trojans. The gods
themselves go down to the plain and interfere more than ever. Aeneas,
encouraged by Apollo, takes on Achilles, but needs Poseidon to rescue him.
Achilles kills Polydorus, Hector's brother, and Apollo then protects Hector when
he is most in danger. Now Achilles seems hardly to dismount from his chariot as
he flies across the plain and drives the Trojans back to the River Scamander.

> The axle-tree beneath
> Was all blood-splashed, and all the rims about
> The chariot, for the blood-drops spattered them
> Both from the horses' hoofs and from the tires.
> But still the son of Peleus hurried on
> To win renown, and his resistless hands
> Were flecked with blood.

Book XX, lines 499–503.

The river, however, *filled with corpses*, rebels. The epic then goes into an unparalleled
description, the struggle between the River Xanthus and the hero Achilles, who
will be given support by the blacksmith god, the god of fire Hephaestus.

Quadriga (black-figured
amphora from the end
of the 4th century BC).

Struggling from the swirl
Achilles in alarm set out to fly
Across the plain with all his speed: but yet
The great god would not cease; he rose at him
In a black crest, and chased divine Achilles
To make him hold his hand, and to preserve
The Trojans from destruction. Peleus's son
Rushed back a spear-throw length with all the speed
Of a black eagle, that great hunter which
Has a strength and pace above all things that fly.
Like him he sped, and on his breast the bronze
Rang grimly, as he swerved to dodge the river
And ran, while on his trail the River came
With a loud roar. And as a channel-maker
Guides from a sunless spring the flow of water
Among his crops and beds, and pick in hand
Clears barriers from the conduit; as it runs,
Before it all the pebbles roll away,
And with a gurgle down the slope apace
It slips, outrunning even him that guides it;
So did the River's deluge still o'ertake
Achilles, racer though he was: the gods
Are forceful beyond men.

Book XXI, lines 246–264.

Water and Fire

Of Gods and Men

STANDARD EPITHETS ARE FREQUENTLY USED TO DESCRIBE the heroes of *The Iliad* as being *like gods* or *divinities*. In their beauty and bravery they are more than ordinary humans. The whole poem nevertheless clearly defines the limits that separate them from the divine world. In Book V, Diomedes had managed to wound two divinities, the fragile goddess of Love and the fearsome Ares, least loved of all

PREVIOUS PAGE
The Wrath of Jupiter, by J.-B. J. Wicar (1762–1834). There is no illustration of the furious river pursuing Achilles: here painting cannot rival poetry. This angry Jupiter conveys the power of the gods when roused to anger.

the gods; but, despite three attempts, he was not able to take on the god Apollo. As the god roared angrily at him, '... *the race of everlasting gods / Is not like that of men who go on earth.*' Achilles too experiences this, as, faced by the river which pursues him *in full flood*, sweeping along *the horde of dead*, his famous swift feet can help him only to flee, in a scene which is like no other in *The Iliad*.

ABOVE
Neptune's Chargers, by Walter Crane (1845–1915). Although this picture also does not feature a river, the famous illustrator clearly shows, in the context of Poseidon, the savage power of the liquid element.

Masters of the Elements

The gods are everywhere and ever-present in the epic, but as a rule they are kept clearly distinct from the natural elements they rule over. Zeus is the master of the heavens, and of thunder and lightning; Poseidon, *the famous Shaker of the earth*, rules over the sea, and Hades, *the monarch of the dead*, over the underworld according to a division which is explicitly described in Book XV. Torrents and river come into the similes, as realities of nature, as does the channel too, though this is a man-made creation. However, in this scene Xanthus is at once a river in flood and a furious god. While this union prefigures the fantastic element found in the Charybdis and Scylla of *The Odyssey*, the characterisation of the river remains, despite everything, close to those of the usual divinities. Its angry reactions are identical to those of humans when their honour is endangered. It appeals to its brother, Simois, to avenge the affront it has suffered, and it requires the intervention of another god, at the request of Hera, to stop a battle between water and fire which paves the way for subsequent theories about pre-Socratic cosmologies relating to the elementary principles of the universe.

Neptune on his chariot (etching, 1595).
This illustration brings together human
figures and allegory in its description
of marine elements in a setting which,
in this case, is very peaceful.

Apollo on His Chariot, by Eugène
Delacroix (1798–1863). Study
for the central group in the
Galerie d'Apollon at the Louvre.

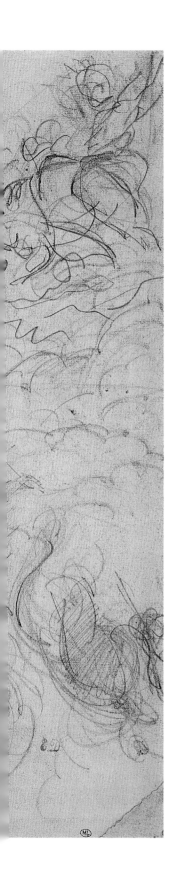

Thereat Hephaestus launched his wondrous fire.
Across the plain it flared up first and burned
The many dead who lay about in heaps,
Slain by Achilles. All the plain was parched,
And the bright water clogged. And as in autumn
The North wind soon dries up an orchard-plot
New-watered, and the husbandman is glad,
So the whole plain dried up; and the dead men
He burned to ash, and then against the River
He turned his blinding flame. The elms were burned,
Burned were the willows and the tamarisks,
The galingales, the lotuses, the rushes
Which grew in plenty by the pleasant streams.
Tormented were the eels and fish beneath
The eddies, and along the pleasant streams
This way and that they dived in their distress
At wise Hephaestus's blast.

Book XXI, lines 342–355.

This fight threatens to unleash a general set-to among the gods, which would
have compromised the order of the world if Apollo had not put an end to it.
What is the good, he said, of fighting for *miserable mortals*? Let them resolve
their own quarrels. Zeus then adjusted the fates of Hector and Achilles, and the
gods abandoned Hector. Athene, however, continued to interfere; she deceived
Hector by disguising herself as his youngest brother and inciting him to fight,
then, at the decisive moment, abandoned him, leaving him alone face to face
with the furious warrior. As a hero, he decides to fight despite everything.
As Jacqueline de Romilly put it so well, one has to see in this 'sudden start of
a man faced with a desperate situation, in which he recognises the divine will
at work' the 'heroism of a man alone' which is Homeric heroism.

And as there goeth in darkness of the night
One star among the others, Hesperus
(The fairest star that in the skies is set),
So shone the spear-head which in his right hand
With sinister intent Achilles shook
At noble Hector, eyeing his fair flesh
To find the weakest spot. All elsewhere he
Was guarded by the brave bronze armour which
He stripped from strong Patroclus when he slew him;
But by the collar-bone midway between
Shoulder and neck or gullet was a gap
Where is the quickest way to take the life:
And there, as Hector charged him, great Achilles
Drove in his spear, and through the tender neck
Clean went the point. And yet the ashen spear
Bronze-weighted, missed the wind-pipe, so that he
Could still speak words of answer to his foe.
Down in the dust he crashed, and great Achilles
Exulted o'er him: 'But thou thoughtest, Hector,
When thou didst spoil Patroclus, thou wast safe,
And hadst no heed to me who kept aloof!
Fool! for away among the hollow ships
Was left a helper mightier far than he,
I, who have loosed thy knees. And dogs and birds
Shall rend thee foully, while the Achaeans hold
The funeral rites for him.'
Then answered Hector of the flashing helm,
His strength all gone: 'I beg thee by thy life,
Thy knees, thy parents, leave me not for dogs
Of the Achaeans by the ships to eat;

The Death
of Hector

But take abundant store of bronze and gold –
My sire and queenly mother will give it thee –
And render back my body to my home,
So that the Trojans and the Trojans' wives
May give my due meed of fire in death.'
But scowling at him swift Achilles said:
'Do not entreat me, dog, by knees or parents.
I only wish I had the heart and will
To hack the flesh off thee and eat it raw,
For all that thou hast done to me! There lives
None who shall keep the dogs away from thee;
Not even if they brought and weighed out here
Ransom ten-fold and twenty-fold, and promised
More thereunto; no, not though Priam, son
Of Dardanus, bid pay thy weight in gold;
Not even so thy queenly mother shall
Lay on a bier and mourn the son she bore,

But dogs and birds shall eat thee utterly.'
Then as he died said Hector of the helm:
'I know thee well; I see thee as thou art;
I was not to persuade thee, for thou hast
An iron heart in thee. But heed thou lest
I bring on thee the anger of the gods
That day when Paris and Apollo too
Shall quell thy valour at the Scaean Gate.'
The end of death closed on him as he spoke;
And fleeting from his limbs his spirit was gone
To Hades' house, bewailing what befell it
And leaving manliness and youth behind.
Dead as he was, to him said great Achilles:
'Lie dead: for me, I will accept my fate
Whenever Zeus and all the immortal gods
Wish to accomplish it.'

Book XXII, lines 317–366.

Death Foretells Death

As in the story of Patroclus's death, several lines of which and the general set of themes are partly repeated here in a way which is certainly intentional, the last words exchanged are more important than the fatal blow, which is described with the poet's usual terrible surgical precision. Here too it is the dying man who sees the truth: Achilles will end up returning Hector's body to Priam, Achilles will die at the hands of Paris, thanks to Apollo, at the gates of Troy. The victor, on the other hand, is at this point carried away by such a warring fury that he allows himself horrible cannibalistic desires: not only shall dogs and birds devour Hector, as the poem foretells in its opening lines, but he himself wants to eat Hector raw, like a Cyclops, a Polyphemus, transferred to the world of heroes.

Savage Violence

Violence in war has two faces. One is seen as positive, the ardour for glorious combat, channelled by discipline and a clear distinction between friends and enemies. The other is negative, the blind fury which leads men to kill beyond measure and reason. That is all the warrior sees. Achilles, *the best of the Achaeans*, is on the brink of becoming a savage. In a state of hubris, violence becomes excess, and leads from anger to madness. The warrior only manages to kill himself. This is what is at stake in the death of Hector, the last and most terrible death in the poem. It is notable that Achilles' final words are spoken after Hector is already dead. Achilles' indifference to his own fate overhangs the work, overhanging *The Iliad*, which reciprocates by not relating this unavoidable destiny which has been accepted in advance. The two final Books are devoted to the consequences of the deaths of Patroclus and Hector, as means of abandoning savage violence and returning to civilised human relationships, thanks to the rituals of grief and reconciliation, even though they are temporary. Book XXIII describes the Achaean camp, after the quarrels, assembled for the solemn cremation of the body of Patroclus, and the games organised in his honour by Achilles. Book XXIV goes much further. First Achilles is seized by a burst of fury and drags the body of Hector around the ramparts of Troy, in full view of his people, but the gods condemn this act, protect the Trojan's body and invite Priam to go, alone, to reclaim his son in Achilles' camp.

PAGE 101
Achilles Dragging the Body of Hector Before the Walls of Troy, Watched by Priam and Hecuba Who Entreat the Victor, by Antoine-François Callet (1741–1823).

PREVIOUS PAGES
The Death of Hector, by Biagio di Antonio (c. 1476–1504).

OPPOSITE
Achilles dragging Hector's body, mosaic from the Vatican Mueum.

OVERLEAF
The furious Achilles cuts the throat of a Trojan beside the funeral pyre of Patroclus (detail from a volute krater by the painter from Darius, 4th century). The episode is described in *The Iliad*, which states that then 'four superb horses' were sacrificed, two of Patroclus's nine dogs and 'twelve noble sons of courageous Trojans', 'for he dreamed only of revenge'.

Then there arose great Aias Telamon,
And up rose deep Odysseus, crafty-souled,
And girding them they stepped into the ring,
And gripped each other close with sinewy hands,
Like gable rafters of a lofty house
Bolted together by some famous builder,
To baffle stormy winds. Their backbones creaked
With the stiff wrenchings of their hardy hands;
The sweat came pouring from them; dark with blood
On rib and shoulder many a wale sprang out,
As still they struggled might and main to win
The hammered tripod. Neither could Odysseus
Trip Aias up and bring him to the ground,
Nor Aias him, for his great strength held out.

Book XXIII, lines 708–720.

The Funeral of Patroclus

ΠΑΤΡΟΚΛΟ   ΤΑΦΟΣ

ΠΑΥΣΙΝ

ΚΥΛΟΡΤΟ

ΣΙΜΑΣΧΟΤ

PREVIOUS PAGES
Javelin throwers and archers (detail from the 'François vase', 570 BC). This famous vase, discovered in 1844 by the painter Alexandre François, is signed with the names of the potter Ergotimos and the painter Cleinias. It shows various epic scenes illustrating the funeral games in honour of Patroclus. This detail is of a famous hunt by the hero Meleager.

ABOVE
Chariot driver. This ceramic, painted at the end of the period known as 'Geometric', was made in the same era that *The Iliad* was probably compiled, c. 710 BC.

The games in honour of Patroclus restored a time of peace, when men only played at combat. These games are, for all that, not without stakes, and here we can see the 'agonal' mentality that our civilisation has inherited from Ancient Greece. According to tradition the Olympic Games, it should be remembered, were inaugurated in 776 BC, or at the time it is generally thought *The Iliad* was composed, and were held without interruption at least until the 3rd century AD. Some of the events described here certainly go back to the Minoan and Mycenaean civilisations.

They begin with the chariot race, the most prestigious event, whose developments occupy some four hundred lines, establishing it as the supreme test of the competition, then come boxing and wrestling, which were also well known, then the running race later known as 'stade', followed by an armed combat, which is more surprising, and finally throwing the discus, archery and throwing the javelin. Achilles presented Agamemnon with the prize for the last contest, even though he had not competed, as a way of bringing their quarrel to a definitive end.

The wrestling match between Ajax and Odysseus introduces Odysseus to this work, the hero 'full of tricks and cunning', a man who is ingenious and perpetually inventive. The poet does not award the contest to either man, which was not without significance for his audiences, who knew the legends of other epics from the Trojan cycle. Ajax is the most valiant warrior after Achilles, but it is Odysseus's ruse which will bring about the fall of Troy. They will confront each other violently after the death of Achilles, to win the honour of recovering his arms. This is awarded to Odysseus, and Ajax, dishonoured, and perhaps in a fit of madness, kills himself. At the end of their fight here, Achilles declares both heroes the winners, which confirms the reconciliatory character of the end of *The Iliad*.

'Do not press it further,
Nor be too hard upon yourselves: ye both
Are winners; take the prizes half and half,
And go, that other Achaeans may be matched.'

Book XXIII, lines 735–737.

Then Spoke Priam and entreated him, and said:
'Remember, O Achilles, like the gods,
Thy father, who is old as I am old,
On the grim threshold of old age. May be
His neighbours round about him grind him down,
And he has none to keep off hurt and harm:
And yet, because he hears that thou art living,
His heart is glad, and every day he hopes
To see his dear son coming home from Troia.
But I, what comfort have I, who begot
The finest sons in all wide Troy, of whom
Not one, I say, is left? Fifty I had
When came the sons of the Achaeans: born
To me were nineteen of the self-same womb,
And women of the palace bore the others.
Fierce Ares loosed the knees of all those many;
But the one left to me, the one who kept
His town and people, fighting for his country,
Lately thou slewest – Hector. For his sake
Here am I come to the Achaeans' ships,
To beg him of thee, and I bring with me
A priceless ransom. Nay, revere the gods,
Achilles, and remembering thy father
Have pity on me; I am more piteous;
I have endured what never mortal man
On earth has yet endured, to stretch my hand
Unto the mouth of him who slew my son.'

Book XXIV, lines 486–506.

The Plea of Priam

The Grief of a Father

THE POEM COULD HAVE ENDED WITH THE DEATH OF HECTOR or the funeral of Patroclus. It seems that the author of *The Iliad* wanted to end it not with death, but, according to the words of one critic, with the restoration of humanity. This restoration is effected by the sharing of tears. The plea of Priam is a ritual act: suppliants, in Greek religion, must be treated with respect and welcomed, whatever they have done. But the reaction of Achilles is not merely a ritual one: he bursts into tears – and *for remembrance both wept bitterly*. The scene recalls the father-son relationship between Achilles and Peleus, and between Hector and Priam, expressing both emotion and solidarity. It also raises the contrast between the living Achilles and the dead Hector: but everyone knows, Achilles most of all, that this contrast is only temporary, which increases the pathos of his reaction. The lesson of these tears can perhaps be found in a sentence written a few centuries later by the historian Herodotus: 'No man is so insane as to prefer war to peace. In peacetime, children bury their fathers; in wartime, fathers bury their children.' In his reply to Priam after he has wept, Achilles adds another lesson, which also has a bearing on humanity, though from a much more general point of view:

For thus it is the gods have spun the thread
For miserable men, to spend their lives
In pain, while they are sorrowless themselves.

Book XXIV, lines 525–526.

Two jars, he says, stand on the floor of Zeus's palace, one containing evil things, the other good. Achilles does not say how Zeus attributes some with a mixture of evil and good, and others with only evil, but this is the underlying idea: destiny is fate, the result of a perpetual lottery between evil and good, and we must resign ourselves to this, and stop endlessly upsetting ourselves. The quest for glory, the leitmotif of *The Iliad*, seems here to be a very fragile substitute for human insecurity.

PREVIOUS PAGE
Priam Begging Achilles to Return the Body of Hector, by Alexander Andreyevich Ivanov (1806–1858).

OPPOSITE
Priam, by Nicolas Poussin (1594–1665).

FOLLOWING PAGES
The companions of Odysseus row hastily away from the Island of the Sirens (detail from a stamnos jar by the painter of the Sirens).

The Odyssey
The Glorious Return

The Adventures of
Telemachus

FÉNELON WROTE 'THE ADVENTURES OF TELEMACHUS' IN
1699 AS PART OF THE EDUCATION OF THE GRANDSON OF
LOUIS XIV. IN 'THE ODYSSEY', THEY ARE JUST AN OPENING
STAGE, SETTING THE FATE OF THE FATHER AGAINST THE
FUTURE OF HIS FAMILY, AND PREPARING THE WAY FOR HIS
RETURN TO ITHACA.

*I pursue the slightest echoes of the great name of my father, the divine
and patient Odysseus.*

Penelope and Telemachus (red-figured
Attic skyphos, or drinking cup, by the
'painter of Penelope', 5th century BC).
On the reverse is the scene where
Eurycleia recognises Odysseus on his
return. Here, Telemachus watches his
mother as she sits in front of the loom,
endlessly weaving her shroud. In these
two paintings, the artist captures the
essential character of the work.

But for Odysseus wise I am ill at ease,
That man unhappy, who amid the seas
Far from his friends affliction bears for long
Within the sea-girt island set with trees;
The island in whose bounds a goddess dwells,
Daughter of Atlas of the guileful spells,
Who holds the lofty pillars of the earth
And heaven apart, and knows the deep sea-wells.
His daughter holds that woeful wretch in thrall,
And with soft flattering speeches therewithal
Lulls his distress, that so of Ithaca
Forgetfulness upon his heart may fall.
But for his island Odysseus longs so sore
That even the smoke upcurling from its shore
Fain would he see and die: yet is your heart,
Lord of Olympus, softened none the more.
Did not Odysseus on the gods bestow
Reward of sacrifices long ago,
Down in wide Troy beside the Argive ships?
Why does your wrath, O Zeus, afflict him so?

Book I, lines 48–62.

Athene, Odysseus and Telemachus

On the Island of Ithaca

ON HIS WAY BACK FROM THE TROJAN WAR, after many adventures which the epic will describe later, Odysseus has ended up alone on the island of the goddess Calypso, who is keeping him prisoner. But he is not the only hero in this work. *The Odyssey* features a harmonious, non-competitive pair of heroes, Odysseus and his son Telemachus. Athene suggests the divine messenger Hermes is sent to see the goddess Calypso to ask for Odysseus's release, while she decides to go, disguised as a friend of Odysseus called Mentes, to encourage Telemachus to set off in search of his father.

The main part of the action takes place in Ithaca, Odysseus's homeland, the present-day Itháki, a small mountainous island near the west coast of central Greece, where Mycenaean remains have been found. Athene arrives on the island from Olympus. In Book II, we set off from there with Telemachus and will return in Book XIII with Odysseus, and remain there. At first in Ithaca we only see the palace, where Penelope's suitors feast shamelessly, then later we discover the countryside, where Odysseus prepares his plans in the pigsty of Eumaeus. Between Book II and Book XIII, we travel first of all in the real world with Telemachus to Pylos, to see Nestor, then to Sparta to see Menelaus. Then we follow Odysseus into the wondrous world of the Mediterranean, which he crossed on his way back from Troy.

The first part of the story deals exclusively with Telemachus. For four Books, we only see Odysseus through what his son knows of him, and through the resemblance between father and son which everyone who meets Telemachus points out. Through Telemachus we also see Penelope, not at first as Odysseus's wife but as a mother: she regards the growing freedom of the young adult with bitterness and sadness. Describing the son as a hero will only make him a rival to his father. The second stage of the story, devoted entirely to Odysseus, leaves no doubt about his heroic nature, and the fact that he really did pass the most severe tests. This paves the way for the third part, in which the father and son – the former leading, the other following, and with help from Penelope – together create a heroic unity of a new kind, celebrating their victory and the recognition of their triumph. Subsidiary characters protect the family's integrity in their vicissitudes: the old nurse Eurycleia, the good servant Eumaeus, who is almost an adopted father to Telemachus, and the faithful dog Argus.

Pallas Athene, by Franz von Stuck
(1863–1928). The wise and kindly goddess
controls the intrigue in the first part of the
book, at first with Zeus in Olympia and
then in Ithaca with Telemachus.

Athene Shows Ithaca to Odysseus, by
Giuseppe Bottani (1717–1784).
'For sweeter than his parents and
his home / Is naught' (Book IX,
lines 34–35).

Athene, Odysseus and Telemachus   123

The Gods and Moral Values

In *The Odyssey*, two divinities control the action, Zeus and his daughter Athene. Poseidon is angry with Odysseus for having shattered the eye of his son, the Cyclops Polyphemus, but can only delay his return to Ithaca. Athene intervenes principally to indicate what should be done to help and provoke action. Before Athene mentioned Odysseus, Zeus was having one of his rare fits of rage against humans, those mortals who never stopped blaming the gods for their misfortunes when they themselves were chiefly responsible.

'Alas, how idly do these mortals blame
The gods, as though by our devising came
The evil that, beyond what was ordained,
By their own folly for themselves they frame!'

Book I, lines 32–34.

Zeus was thinking in particular of the lover of Clytemnestra, Aegisthus, the murderer of King Agamemnon, who had just been killed by Orestes, the king's son. Quite, replies Athene, but Odysseus is not like him at all, he is not responsible for any of his misfortunes: we should therefore help the son of Laertes. Here we are a very long way from the Zeus who casually draws from the two jars of good and evil things. The problem of man's misfortune is here given a solution that for the first time is theologically satisfactory: evil men and madmen, and they alone, will be punished. Odysseus is the virtuous equivalent of Agamemnon, and Penelope that of Clytemnestra: they will be rewarded. The suitors, vainly pursuing Penelope and ruining Odysseus's household, are the equivalent of Aegisthus and will be punished.

The moral of the story is further reinforced by a second contrast, between Odysseus and his companions. Contrary to what happens in *The Iliad*, fury does not lead the hero to excesses, nor does it modify the realisation of the original plan, overseen as it is by Athene and protected by her cunning and intelligence. It is his companions on the voyage back from Troy who embody stupidity and disrespect for normal behaviour, and they are punished for it, as the poet declares in the prologue. Their fate arouses more pity than condemnation, and draws from it a wholly positive lesson: intelligence, endurance and good behaviour are rewarded by success.

OPPOSITE
Athene and her flying owl (detail from a red-figured Etruscan vase, c. 360 BC). Through Athene, patroness of Athens, the owl became the city's emblem, symbolising intelligence and watchfulness. On the right is the trident of Poseidon, the only god in Olympus who for a time was against Odysseus.

The Suitors

The suitors consist of a hundred or so lords of Ithaca and the surrounding islands who take their name from the fact that they hope to win the hand of Penelope. Why are they courting her? The answer is not entirely clear. Most of all they covet Odysseus's title of King of Ithaca, and perhaps also his estate: twelve herds of beef and sheep on the mainland, and eleven herds of goats and several hundred pigs on the island itself. If one of them were to win the title, Penelope would presumably have to leave Odysseus's palace and return to her father with all the assets she had brought with her as her dowry, and choose another husband. There was another possibility: for her to marry one of them in Odysseus's palace, as Clytemnestra married Aegisthus. Penelope rejects these options, while her son grows up and every day threatens more strongly to take his father's place, which would ruin all their hopes.

The suitors are very often described in a collective fashion, as a group of arrogant idlers full of excesses and violence, and that overweening nature that the Greeks called *hybris*. This mainly entails a lack of respect for the rules governing social relationships among the aristocracy, especially two of these, the organisation of banquets and hospitality. In peacetime, feasts were one of the principal ways of demonstrating and maintaining the status and honourable position of an aristocrat, whether they were organised by people of the same world, by invitation, or by sharing expenses, or given to the people. But the suitors spend their time in debauched banqueting at someone else's house, in Odysseus's palace, and gradually 'devour' his patrimony: no one invited them, they never return hospitality, their feasts follow no ritual sacrifice, nor do they contribute in any way to the meals they eat. Furthermore, they completely ignore the rules of hospitality, recognised by the community of lords across local boundaries: they require that every *xenos* (the Greek word means both stranger and guest) be welcomed and given food before he is asked who he is; if he is a guest of the family or an important person, he will be treated magnificently and given lavish presents.

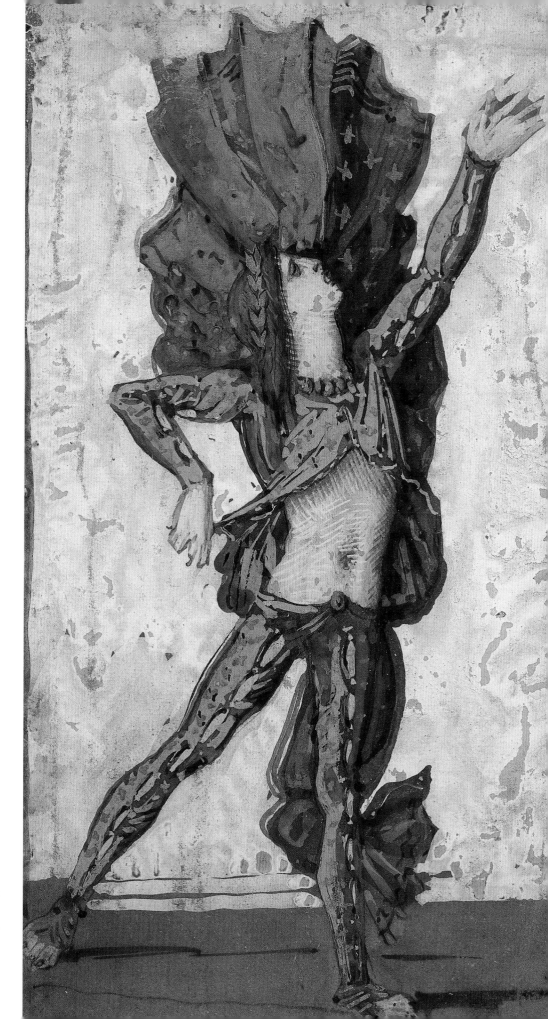

Study for *The Suitors*, by Gustave
Moreau (1826–1898).
This sketch for a large painting,
which Moreau did not complete,
conveys the Symbolist painter's
fascination with the utterances
of the suitors, and the effect they
had on his refined and rather
morbid imagination.

Telemachus and Athene Disguised as
Mentor, by Karl Bauer (1868–1942).
This drawing illustrated a poem
inspired by the story of Telemachus,
Nocturnal Voyage by Conrad Ferdinand
Meyer (1825–1898).

Athene in Disguise

Telemachus, as a worthy son of Odysseus, welcomes Mentes as he should, and does not recognise the goddess Athene. She sings his praises: *'Your head and your bright eyes like his appear'*, while Telemachus is hesitant about his true identity: *'My mother says I am his son: but I / Know not; who ever his begetting knew?'* Then Athene criticises the behaviour of the suitors:

'But tell me now, and let your words be clear,
What concourse, what carousal have we here?
Banquet or bridal? what is your part therein?
For not at common cost is this good cheer.
So insolent and masterful the throng
Meseems that feasting sit your hall along.
Sure, if a wise man entered well might he
Be wroth, beholding all this shame and wrong.'

Book I, lines 224–229.

The conflict with the suitors has been set up and now it explodes. Mentes advises the young man boldly to send the suitors home at a public meeting of the people of Ithaca. To Penelope's stupefaction, Telemachus drily orders his mother to go up to her room (for *speech shall stand / for men to handle*), and summons the meeting, which the suitors attend, though much taken aback by this bold venture. The meeting is not a democratic assembly where everyone may speak, but a kind of public debate between the principal elders of the city, held in front of the crowd. Then, after Telemachus's speech, the leading suitor, Antinous, vents his anger and replies with a brutal and categorical refusal.

'Nowise the Achaean wooers are to blame;
But your own mother, by whose cunning sleight
Three years are fled and now the fourth takes flight,
Wherein the hearts of the Achaean lords
She vexes, holding hope out to their sight:
And flattering messages to each and all
Sends, with intent that they may fruitless fall.
And this guile likewise in her heart she planned,
When a great loom she built within her hall,
And wrought thereon a broad web woven fine,
Saying to us: O youthful wooers mine,
Since dead is bright Odysseus, cease awhile
My heart to hasty marriage to incline,
Until this web be finished, lest I leave
A labour spoiled the weaving that I weave,
A shroud for burial of the aged prince
Laertes: since it verily would grieve
Full many Achaean women in the town,

Penelope
and the Suitors

If shroudless he should lie, who had renown
For wealth of his own gathering, when the doom
Of Death the Leveller shall strike him down.
So spake she: and, as is the way of men,
We were persuaded. All the daytime then
At the great loom she wove, and every night
With torches set unwove her work again.
Thus for the space of full three years did she
Deceive the Achaeans by her subtlety;
But when the fourth year brought the seasons round,
One of her maids revealed the mystery.
And we the bright web on the loom that lay
Found her unravelling: wherefore from that day
Perforce she needs must bring it to an end.
Now thus the wooers make reply and say,
That both yourself in your own mind may know,
And all the Achaeans: bid your mother go,
And let her marry him among us all
Whom her sire bids, and her it pleases so.
But if the sons of the Achaeans still
She vexes by the counsel of her will –
Seeing that Athena has bestowed on her
Wisdom of mind and excellence of skill
In beautiful devices manifold

Beyond all others, such as is not told
Even of those renowned in former time,
Achaean lovely-tressed of old,
Tyro, Alcmena, and Mycena crowned;
Even among these the equal was not found
In wise devices to Penelope:
Yet now her wit has overleapt the bound.
And therefore these men will not cease to slay
Your cattle, and your substance waste away,
So long as she the selfsame purpose keeps
That in her heart the gods have set today;
To win vainglory for herself, but ill
For you and damage: to the lands we till
Return we will not, nor depart at all,
Ere she wed one among us, whom she will.
But wise Telemachus made answer thus:
'Ill were it done of me, Antinous,
To thrust her from my doors against her will
Who bore and nursed me, while afar from us
Alive or dead, my father to this day
Is gone [...] But for you,
If you take shame at all this wrong you do,
Quit these my halls; henceforward turn by turn
Array the banquet your own houses through!'

Book II, lines 87–132, 138–140.

Penelope Weaving the Shroud of Laertes, Her Father-in-law,
While Waiting for her Husband Odysseus to Return, by
Max Klinger (1857–1920). Here Klinger shows
a Penelope who is the mistress of the world, of life
and death, in a mysterious and dreamlike atmosphere
that appealed to Symbolists and Surrealists.

Penelope's Web

PENELOPE IS THE FEMALE COUNTERPART OF ODYSSEUS. She matches the inventive and ingenious man with her feminine astuteness and intelligence. Much later, Penelope will again, and with some pride, tell the story of her famous ruse to Odysseus though she has not yet recognised him. Finally, in the last Book, the suitors, in the underworld, will return to the trick she played on them.

In the world of the epic, the main occupation of women, especially women in high society, is to weave on a large vertical loom: the queens Helen of Sparta and Arete of Phaeacia are also at their looms when the poet introduces them. Until classical times, it was one of the great contributions they made to the life of their household and their city. The activity of weaving, with its crisscrossing of threads and the slow creation of complex motifs, suggests intelligence and cunning, everything that creates a 'web' (the image lives on to this day) of human ingenuity. In Ancient Greece and elsewhere, women are also associated with wiliness, with the slow formulation of ruses that are 'hatched' over a long period. Penelope's trick has a paradoxical character which made her famous: what she 'weaves' is in fact to unravel during the night the web she built up during the day.

The Departure of Telemachus

The time references given here suggest that the suitors did not move into Odysseus's palace immediately after the end of the Trojan war, but only five or six years later. This still means that Penelope tricked them for more than four years.

The words of Antinous, the leading suitor and the most violent of them all, are quite clear: he speaks with authority. The situation has reached a breaking point. Despite the pleas of Telemachus, and the prophetic appearance of two eagles, representing a sign in his favour, the suitors control the meeting and end it without anyone protesting. Telemachus is even forbidden to put to sea.

So now he too must hide his intentions. With the help of his nurse Eurycleia, he prepares for his departure without even informing his mother, and, during the night, reaches the coast of the Peloponnese.

And the sun left the lovely lake and rose
Upward across the sky's brass-paved dome,
To light the deathless gods, and mortal men
That have the acres of the corn for home.
And they to Pylos, Nestor's city trim,
Came: where the people, down by the sea's brim,
Made to the blue-haired Shaker of the Earth
Oblation, slaying coal-black bulls to him.
Nine rows of seats, and in each of these
Five hundred men, set after their degrees,
Offered nine bulls: and while on the offal meat
They fed, and burned to god the thigh-pieces,
These in their balanced ship drew straight to land,
And furled the sails and moored her by the strand.
Then out they got, and out Telemachus
Came at the leading of Athena's hand.

Book III, lines 1–12.

The Voyages of Telemachus

The Sacrifices in Nestor's City

BEYOND ITHACA, THE WORLD THAT TELEMACHUS discovers is ordered and beautiful, as the image of the rising sun immediately suggests, then the perfect organisation of the sacrifice made on the beach by the Pylians in honour of the god Poseidon, the grandfather of King Nestor. This book ends with another sacrifice which is even more solemn. Unlike life on Pylos, banquets on Ithaca did not include sacrifices, which elsewhere in Greek civilisation were indispensable before any beef dishes were eaten. The suitors, in contrast, were sacrilegious. One of Hesiod's myths tells how the ritual of sacrifice came about. When the Titan Prometheus was made responsible for dividing up the parts of the carcass between the gods and men, he is supposed to have given Zeus the worst parts, the bones and the fat, and men the best, the meat and the offal. He also managed to give men fire. The king of the gods responded to this by forcing men to work the land and live off it, sending them the beautiful Pandora (with her famous box or 'jar'), the source of all their misfortunes, particularly from women. The sacrifice of the oxen is thus not only a means of eating meat, it implies order in the world: the division between beasts, gods and men, the need for work and the division of humanity into two sexes.

Unmarked animals were selected for sacrifice, black ones for the underworld gods (with whom Poseidon was associated) and white ones for the celestial gods. They were sprayed with a purifying lustral water and barley seed, some hairs were removed and burnt, their necks were severed with an axe and raised up so the throat could be cut. The blood was collected in a vase and spilled on the open-air altar as an offering to the gods. Then, following a very precise ritual, the beast was sliced up, the offal and the meat roasted on the fire and shared round. The ceremony was performed with no specialist clergy present, the nobles themselves taking part in every stage of the cult. The killing was accompanied by the prayers of the participants and the wailing of women.

PREVIOUS PAGE
Sacrificial scene (detail from a red-figured Attic bell krater, 430 BC). While the meat on the spit is roasted, a bearded priest seems to be offering a flatbread, while a young man carrying a ritual basket pours out a libation.

FOLLOWING PAGES
The Trojan Horse, by Tamas Galambos (1994).

The Story of the Trojan Horse

The voyages of Telemachus are both a lesson in devotion and in hospitality. The welcome he receives from Nestor, and then from Menelaus, is perfect. The feasts given in his honour give us a picture of how the Trojan war ended and the various heroes returned home, which sets up the story of Odysseus's return. In Sparta, particularly, in the luxurious palace of Menelaus and Helen, we hear a curious anecdote about the famous trick of the Trojan horse. In these lines, Menelaus is addressing Helen.

'Whereof now likewise may this tale find room,
How we, within the carved horse's womb,
The Argive princes lay, intent to bear
Upon the Trojans violent death and doom;
And how you then came thither, being sent
Belike by prompting of some god who meant
To glorify the Trojans; and withal
Godlike Deiphobus beside you went.
Then thrice round the hollow gin you came,
And touched it with your hands, and called by name
Each of the Argive princes; and your voice
To each was as his own wife's voice the same.
But all amid them Tydeus's son and I
And bright Odysseus sat and heard your cry,
Then both we two were fain to issue forth
Or from within at once to make reply.
But then Odysseus checked us, fain to fall
Into the snare, and kept in silence all
The Achaean captains: only Anticlus
Yet made essay to answer your call:
Then rose Odysseus's mighty hands and lay
Merciless on his mouth, and saved that day
All the Achaeans, and so held him down
Until Athena led your feet away.'

Book IV, lines 271–289.

The Lost Epic

The fall of Troy was the subject of a lost epic, the *Ilioupersis*. This is the story: 'Odysseus had the idea of making a wooden horse and suggested it to Epeius, who was an architect. He, using wood from Mount Ida, made a hollowed-out horse, with openings in its sides. Odysseus persuaded fifty gallant men to enter the horse; the rest of the Greeks were to burn their camp, put out to sea, moor at Tenedos and return the following night. The Greeks followed his plan and the gallant fighters climbed into the horse, which now bore this inscription: "For their return home, the Greeks have dedicated this offering to Athene as a sign of gratitude." When daylight came, and the Trojans saw the Greeks had deserted their camp, they thought they had fled. They were very happy, and dragged the horse into the city and left it close to Priam's palace, then they began to consider what they should do with it.' (Apollodorus, *The Library*, translated by J.-C. Carrière). Despite the warnings of Cassandra and the soothsayer Lacoon, whose children were devoured by a sea serpent sent to deceive the Trojans, the horse remained in Troy and, when night fell, the city was taken.

The anecdote told here is strange. Clearly, the poet wished to add a new episode to the story which he picks up later in Book VIII. Helen, with Deiphobus, the husband who replaced Paris after his death, was playing an enigmatic game. She seems to have guessed the presence of the Greek heroes, and for each of them her voice magically embodies that of their absent wife. Their desire and nostalgia are so sharply felt that, without Odysseus, they would have betrayed themselves. The story once again shows the power of amorous desire (though limited to relations between married people!), and above all the restraint of Odysseus, who saves the situation. This indicates one of his main characteristics when he returns from Troy, his capacity to hide his feelings and resist amorous inclinations.

'The Trojan Horse', taken from the *Collection of Trojan Stories* by Raoul Le Febvre, 1464. In 1354, an ambassador from the Byzantine emperor to the Papal Court showed the poet Petrarch a copy of *The Iliad*, which the latter kissed, but then said: 'Your Homer does not speak to me,' because he did not know any Greek. Petrarch then had the first modern translations of *The Iliad* and *The Odyssey* made in Latin, which he was still annotating when he died in 1374.

La porte Dardane

Penelope, by Sir Frank Dicksee
(1853–1928).

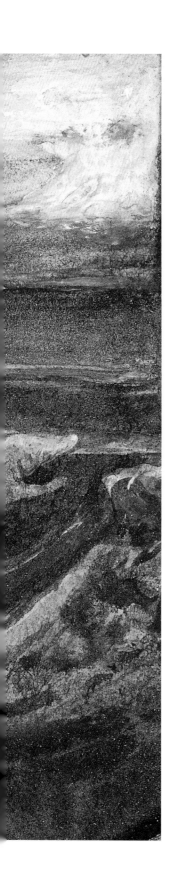

Penelope Without Her Son

Homer now takes us back to Ithaca, where the herald Medon tells Penelope that
her son has left and that the suitors want to kill him. The voyages of Telemachus
end with the pathetic picture of his abandoned mother; a woman without a
husband or a son is bereft of everything.

But bitter anguish at her heartstrings tore,
And on a seat she brooked to sit no more,
Of many that the house was furnished with;
But on the richly fashioned chamber's floor
Moaning in lamentable wise she clung,
While round her wailed the women, old and young,
All of her household: and Penelope
Bitterly sighing spake her maids among:
'Hearken, my women! for upon my head
Surely the Lord Olympian grief has shed
Exceeding great, beyond the lot of all
The women whom this age has born and bred.
For I long since my noble husband lost,
The lion-hearted, in the Danaan host
Renowned for all achievement, and his fame
All over Hellas and mid-Argos crossed.
And now again my own beloved son
The winds have snatched from home, and tidings none
Had I, nor knew I of his setting forth.'

Book IV, lines 716–728.

The Voyages <br> of Odysseus

ODYSSEUS LEAVES THE ISLAND OF CALYPSO, WHERE HE HAD
BEEN KEPT FOR SEVEN YEARS, AND LANDS IN PHAEACIA. IN THIS
WONDERFUL COUNTRY, HE TELLS OF HIS WANDERINGS AND
THOSE OF HIS COMPANIONS ON THEIR WAY BACK FROM TROY:
THE LOTUS EATERS, THE CYCLOPES, THE ISLAND OF AEOLIA,
THE LAESTRYGONIANS, CIRCE, HADES, THE SIRENS, SCYLLA
AND CHARYBDIS, AND THE ISLAND OF THE SUN.

Odysseus's Ship, by Monia (20th century). The boat which Odysseus built with such ingenuity in order to leave Calypso could not withstand the storm sent by Poseidon, furious at the suffering Odysseus had caused his son, the Cyclops Polyphemus. Here the artist seems to evoke both the hero's achievement and the fury of the elements.

6

... and after they had fed
To quench their thirst and hunger, then began
Calypso, bright of goddesses, and said:
'Son of Laertes, high-born, subtle-souled
Odysseus, may your longing naught withhold
To your own land so straightway to be gone?
Then fare you well; but had your heart foretold
How many woes the fates for you decree
Before you reach your country, here with me
You had abode, and in this house had kept,
And been immortal, howso fain to see
That wife for whom through all the days you pine:
Yet deem I not her beauty more than mine.
Since hardly mortal woman may compare
In shape and beauty with my race divine.'
Then in his wisdom spoke and answered he:
'Goddess and mistress, be not wroth with me
Herein: for very well myself I know
That, set beside you, wise Penelope
Were far less stately and less fair to view,
Being but mortal woman, nor like you
Ageless and deathless: but yet even so
I long and yearn to see my home anew.' [...]
He spoke, and the sun dipped, and darkness fell.
And to the hollow cavern's inner cell
They passed, and took delight of love therein,
While each beside the other yet might dwell.

Book V, lines 201–220, 225–227.

Odysseus
Leaves Calypso

Odysseus's Choice

THE GODDESS CALYPSO 'HID' (IN GREEK, *CALYPTO*) ODYSSEUS. The cavern where they embraced each night echoes this confinement, and the element of forced pleasure. In the daytime, it was quite different, with Odysseus *on the headland, his heart bursting with tears*, which the poet sketched in at the beginning of the epic, and which describes his true situation.

When Hermes arrives to tell Calypso of the gods' decision, she protests, but in vain. The die is cast and Calypso must obey. But she is the one who conveys the news to Odysseus, and in their final discussion it seems as though the final decision rests with Odysseus, as if his departure is a personal choice. It is a good example of the double motivation behind heroic acts in epic stories: generally, these are both imposed by the gods and then seen as free choices. This sets the discussion on another level. Calypso's arguments are twofold: misfortune awaits Odysseus if he goes, but he could stay with her for ever, and she is so much more beautiful than Penelope. Odysseus is both cunning and heroic: he accepts both arguments, and turns them into arguments for leaving. Certainly, Penelope is less beautiful, but she is a mortal: here the implication is that he too is a mortal and must accept his mortal condition. Certainly, too, he will encounter misfortune, but his fate, which he must accept, is to go from one test to another. His choice is therefore the conscious one of a mortal, even though it involves enduring misfortune.

The Test of the Storm

In four days, Odysseus builds a raft (another test of his intelligence) and leaves. The promised misfortune is quick to happen. Poseidon, the sea god, sends him a terrible storm, which destroys his raft and forces him to drift for two days on a beam, clothed in a magic veil that a sea-goddess sends him at a crucial moment. Thanks to Athene, he gets close to the shore, but the surf prevents him from landing. Then he decides to hang onto a passing rock with all his strength.

PAGE 149
Odysseus and Calypso, by Max Beckmann (1884–1950). Here the painter seems rather humorously to be combining the figures of Calypso and Circe, the two enchantresses who kept Odysseus in their beds without making him forget Penelope or his kingdom of Ithaca.

PREVIOUS PAGES
The Island of Calypso and Cactus, by Michael Chase (20th century).

A great wave lifted him and bore him in
Upon a jagged rock, that there and then
Had shattered all his bones and stripped his skin,
But that the goddess with the eyes of grey,
Athena, put it in his heart to lay
Both hands tight-clutched upon the rock, and there
Cling gasping till the great wave passed away.
Over his head it went, but backward whirled
Bore down on him and struck him full and hurled
Far out to sea: as when an octopus
Out of its hole is dragged with suckers curled
And clinging round the pebbles of its bed,
So from his mighty hands the skin was shred
Against the rocks; and in the whelming wave
Quite hidden, then Odysseus had been dead
Before his day, in grievous wise and grim,
But that grey-eyed Athena put in him
Counsel, uprising from beneath the flood
That burst upon the land, far out to swim,
Still keeping on the land a sidelong eye
Some shoaling beach or haven to descry.

Book V, lines 425–442.

The octopus is often featured in Greek ceramics from Minoan times onwards. They are very familiar to the Greeks, and their tentacles are frequently found decorating the bellies of vases. The comparison of Odysseus and an octopus has no equivalent in *The Iliad*. It is naturally more suited to the hero's adventures at sea than to the Trojan war. It focuses our attention on the hero's bloody hands, for while an octopus can pull off pebbles when it is torn from a rock, Odysseus has to leave pieces of his own flesh behind, and in so doing shows even greater endurance than an octopus. Although the surf is even more powerful, there still remains this terrible image of a hero ready to put up with anything in order to survive.

Until they reached the lovely river's flow,
Where never-failing water brims the pools,
Bright and abundant gushing from below,
Soilure to cleanse however deep in grain:
And there, the mules unyoking from the wain
Beside the eddying river, turned them loose
To graze the honeyed herbage of the plain.
Then from the cart their hands among
They fetched and into the dark water flung,
And trod them in the trenches busily
Contending: but when all were washed and wrung,
By the seashore they spread them on a reach
Where the waves cleanest washed the pebbled beach.
And now, when they had bathed and oiled themselves,
In the hot sun they left the clothes to bleach,
While by the river bank they sat and fed.
But when their hearts with food were comforted
Their kerchiefs they undid to play at ball:
And in the game white-armed Nausicaa led.
Artemis's self, the Arrow-showerer, so
Rejoices on the mountain side to go
All down the long slope of Taygetus
Or Erymanthus, while before her bow
Wild boar and fleetfoot deer flee fast away,

Odysseus
and Nausicaa

And round her move the wildwood nymphs at play,
Daughters of Zeus the lord of thunder-clouds;
And Leto joys at heart: for fair are they,
Yet fairest of them all the child she bred;
And over all the rest her brows and head
Rise, easily known among them: even so
Among her women shone the maid unwed.
But when for faring homeward she was fain
To fold the fair clothes up, and yoke the wain,
The grey-eyed goddess counsel took once more
That now Odysseus might awake again,
And see the fair maid who his way should tell
On to the town where the Phaeacians dwell.
Thereat the princess to a handmaiden
Threw the ball wide, and missed her, and it fell
In a deep eddy. From them all outbroke
A long shrill cry: and bright Odysseus woke;
And sitting up he pondered inwardly:
'O me! what land is this of mortal folk?
Are these fierce savages and men of blood,
Or hospitable and of godly mood?
And are these voices as of womenkind,
That echo round me now, the maiden brood

Of nymphs who haunt the crags that top the hill
And grassy meads and fountains of the rill?
Or am I nigh to folk of human speech?
Come, for myself now make essay I will.'
So saying, bright Odysseus from his bed
Crept, and from off the bushy thicket shred
A leafy bough to hide his nakedness,
And like a lion on the mountains bred
Strode forth, that, in his might of none in awe,
With eyes afire, through rain and gusty flaw
Goes hunting after the wild woodland deer,
Or sheep or oxen: for his hungry maw
Even the fenced yard where the flocks are pent
Bids him adventure: so Odysseus went
Among the fair-tressed maids to cast himself,
Though naked: for his need was imminent.
Dreadful to them the sea-stained man drew nigh:
And up and down they ran dispersedly
Along the jutting beaches: only then
The daughter of Alcinous did not fly:
Such courage put Athena in her breast:
Unfaltering she stood up and undistressed,
And faced him.

Book VI, lines 85–140.

Arrival in Phaeacia

With the help of the gods Odysseus finally reaches the shore and rests in a thicket, *as at some lone steading far inland / In the black ashes a man hides a brand / … And needs must keep a seed of fire at hand.* He has landed in Phaeacia, without knowing it. Athene then sets up his next journey, appearing in a dream to Nausicaa, the king's daughter, and suggesting that at her age she will soon find a husband, and so she should prepare for her wedding by washing all her finery at the washing-place down by the sea. Nausicaa is very moved by this dream. She asks her father for a team of mules so she can, she says, prepare for the weddings (those of her brothers, she claims, for *maiden shame / To her own father marriage might not name*). Alcinous understands, without needing any further explanation, and agrees. Everything is now ready for the meeting of Odysseus and the beautiful young girl. It is phrased in the context of a possible marriage, but everyone knows, except Nausicaa and the Phaeacians, that this is a red herring.

The Virgin and the Lion

In this extraordinary portrayal of the young girl at the washing-place, everything points to her virginity, which here is identified with purity. The water is clear, the laundry is washed, the girls bathe and anoint themselves with oil. Nausicaa, the *virgo intacta*, is compared to the goddess Artemis, the virgin daughter of Zeus and Leto, and the sister of Apollo. Her grace and lightness are other attributes of her virginity, the carefree nature of the ball game which at the same time is a dance. The young Nausicaa knows nothing of the cares of life: she knows nothing of what the Greeks call the 'yoke' of marriage, and she is still 'fearless' (this is the literal meaning of the Greek adjective). She is a princess, a distinguished person like Artemis, but she is also wild, like the animals that accompany the goddess in the mountains of the Peloponnese.

On the one hand there is her cleanliness and gaiety, on the other the filth and suffering of Odysseus. The contrast is absolute and sets up the role of Nausicaa and her companions: to help Odysseus to move from the wild world into civilised surroundings, to help him wash away the grime of the sea and dress

The Servants of Nausicaa, by Rupert
Charles Wolston Bunny (1864–1947).

him in clean clothes. Homer compares him to a lion, as in *The Iliad*, but the difference is very clear, and is not without its humour. This is not about describing a bloody fight, but Odysseus meeting some young girls. And the lion trembles, is afraid he might be falling among savages or redoubtable divinities. The meeting of Odysseus and Nausicaa is effected by means of the lost ball. We might wonder if Homer is not playing here with another use of the ball motif, which later became a feature of love poetry: *One day fair-haired Love / Hurled a crimson ball at me / It wanted to start a game / With a child in embroidered sandals* (Anacreon). The meeting of Odysseus and Nausicaa very delicately takes up the theme of a young girl's possible marriage. Odysseus wishes to *hide his nakedness*, and the poet plays with the implications. The hero addresses the young girl from a distance, and does not embrace her knees (a traditional gesture of pleading) except verbally, so as not to disturb her modesty. Finally, he hopes she will find a husband she gets on well with. After Nausicaa has given Odysseus the means to wash himself and clean clothes to wear, she suggests taking him to the city, but at a distance, on condition that he walks by himself once the city is in sight, so that no one will suspect her of going elsewhere to find herself a man:

> Proud-hearted are our people; and of them,
> Meeting us, thus might say some baser one:
> 'And who is this, the stranger tall and gay
> That here beside Nausicaa takes his way?
> And where may she have found him? Aye, no doubt
> She brings a husband back with her today! [...]
> As I myself would think it shame,
> If any other girl in suchlike way
> While her own parents lived, should go astray
> In a man's company, and regard them not,
> Nor wait for marriage in the face of day.

Book VI, lines 273–277, 286–288.

Phaeacia, a Model City

And there grow fruit-trees flourishing and great:
Pear-trees and pomegranates, and apple-trees
Laden with shining apples, and by these,
Sweet-juiced figs and olives burgeoning.
Whose fruiting ceases not nor perishes
Winter or summer, all the year; for there
The western breezes ever soft and fair
Ripen one crop and bring another on.
Apple on apple growing, pear on pear,
Grape-bunch on grape-bunch, fig on fig they lie. [...]
And there two springs gush forth, and of the two
One is divided all the garden through,
And one beneath the courtyard gateway runs
Toward the high house: from it the townsfolk drew.
Such glorious gifts the gods that house had lent.
There toilworn bright Odysseus stood intent.

Book VII, lines 114–121, 129–133.

The city of the Phaeacians, the first Utopia in Western literature, is contrasted with Ithaca and the wild countries visited by Odysseus. Harbours, public spaces, ramparts, a royal palace – its structures are admirable. King Alcinous has a wife he reveres, as do all his people. He feasts and governs in happy accord with the princes of Phaeacia. The palace garden is a real paradise. The description of this garden is paralleled by the spontaneous generosity of nature found in other stories about the origins of humanity, in the Golden Age. In this perfect land, guests are welcomed whole-heartedly. Nausicaa's parents offer Odysseus food and shelter, without initially asking him a single question. The queen has naturally recognised the clothes he is wearing. Odysseus then relates the last part of his adventures, but he does not reveal his name. Alcinous declares that if Odysseus wished to settle in Phaeacia, he would not hesitate to give him his daughter in marriage. But Odysseus's departure is arranged for the next day, on a ship provided for him by the Phaeacians.

FOLLOWING PAGES
Landscape beside a river.
Cycladean art.

The Loves of Ares and Aphrodite

While the ship is being made ready, Alcinous organises a feast in honour of their
guest, which includes sporting and musical tests, framed by three songs by the bard
Demodocos. The second of these is an entertainment, the story of the trap set by
the blacksmith god Hephaestus for his wife Aphrodite and her lover Ares.
This episode, known as 'The Loves of Ares and Aphrodite', was severely condemned
by moralists and philosophers, but it won over many painters and poets, for the
network of threads set by the blacksmith god somehow fixes the adulterous union
like a daring snapshot.

'Lord Zeus and blessed deathless gods each one,
Come hither! see what mocking deeds are done
Intolerable, by this child of Zeus
Who me the Haltfoot holds in honour none,
And loves destroying Ares [...]
Now shall you see how these two lovers lie
Beneath my blankets: sore at heart am I.
Yet for a while I think they will not now
Lie thus again, although their love be high.
Soon will both to sleep no more be fain.
But I will hold them by my craft and chain,
Till all the wedding gifts I gave her sire
For that fair wanton he return again [...]
He spoke, and to the bronze-paved hall in haste
Gathered the gods: the helper Hermes came;
Poseidon, he who holds the earth embraced,
Came, prince Apollo the Far-reacher came.
But the she-goddesses abode for shame
Each in her dwelling. In the porch the gods,
Givers of blessing, stood, and like a flame
Unquenchable their laughter rose to see
The craft Hephaestus wrought by subtlety.

Book VIII, lines 306–309, 313–317, 321–327.

Vulcan Showing His Prisoners Mars and Venus to the Gods, by Maerten van Heemskerck (1498–1574). The title of the painting gives the gods their Latin names, but it is contemporary with the rediscovery in France of Ancient Greek, and Dorat, one of the leading professors of Ancient Greek, gave the Collège Royal (the future Collège de France) famous allegorical interpretations of Homer. It was also the time when the first translations of prose and poetry were carried out.

Socrates said to Plato that this story of the chains, when Hephaestus catches Ares with Aphrodite, should not be read to young people, nor should the scene of Zeus being deceived by Hera in *The Iliad*, for such stories do not teach temperance. Thus a link was made between the two episodes, both of which are good-humoured descriptions of the gods' irrepressible bursts of passion. But one of them involves the king of the gods and the outcome of the Trojan war is at stake. The other would be an ordinary act of adultery, almost banal, if it had not taken place in Olympia and did not once more bring together love and war, and if it had not ended with the blacksmith husband taking shrewd revenge. Really, Ares and Aphrodite are made to look ridiculous, but the lame Hephaestus is equally ridiculous, as is revealed by the *unquenchable laughter* of the gods whom the cuckold has unwisely invited to watch him being betrayed.

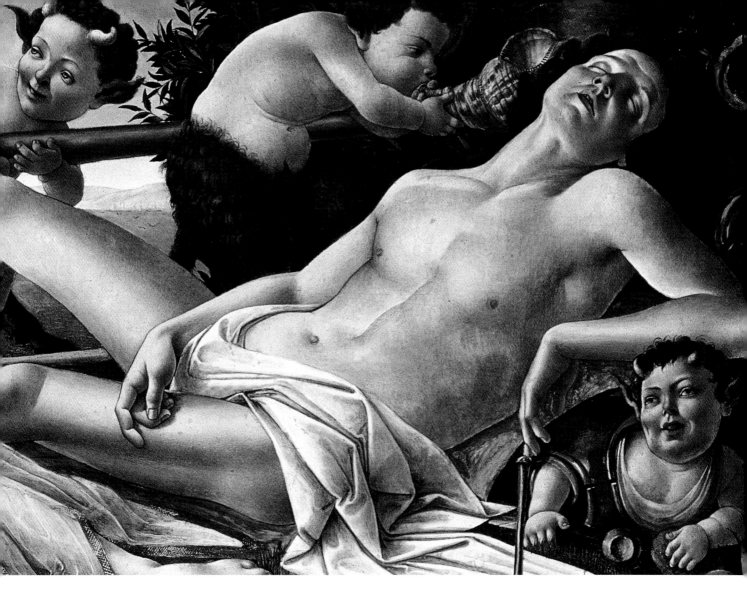

Apart from this passage, there are hardly any other mentions of this ill-matched couple, Aphrodite and Hephaestus. Nonetheless, the episode is perhaps less immoral than Plato claimed. Relations between married couples are a key element in *The Odyssey*: Odysseus had just said to Nausicaa that *there is nothing better in the world,* and Homer had painted a touching picture of Alcinous and his dignified wife. Adultery is severely condemned on several occasions through references to the story of Clytemnestra. Even the idea that Penelope could think of marrying one of the suitors seems incongruous. Relations between Odysseus and Nausicaa are highly restrained. This comical episode with Aphrodite and Hephaestus agreeably confirms the epic's general approval of human fidelity.

Venus and Mars, by Sandro Botticelli (1444–1510). The Florentine artist may be alluding here to the loves of Giuliano de Medici, but this mythological composition, painted in the typically Humanist style of the Italian Renaissance, chiefly shows the victory of love over war: small Cupids hold the lance, and Mars (Ares) is under love's spell.

Odysseus at the Court of Alcinous, King of the Phaeacians, by Francesco Hayez (1791–1882). One of the first paintings in the Neoclassical style.

The Tears of Odysseus

When Demodocos sings about the Trojan war, the tears of Odysseus are
contrasted with the laughter of the eternal gods. This is why Alcinous again asks
him, now more insistently, the question that his wife had already asked: who
are you? what is your name?

'And say why inwardly you weep and wail
To hear what anguish was to Troy assigned
And the Argive Danaans: which things all were done
By operation of the gods, who spun
For men the web of ruin, that thereof
Through ages yet to be a song might run.' [...]
'I will declare, that I hereafter may,
Having escaped from out the evil day,
A friend of yours be reckoned, though from yours
The home wherein I dwell be far away.
Odysseus am I, of Laertes sprung,
Whose wiles mid all men pass from tongue to tongue
And my fame reaches heavenward; and I dwell
In far-seen Ithaca the waves among.
Therein is one fair mountain clad with trees,
Neriton: and all around amid the seas
Nigh one another many isles are set,
Dulichium and Same, and by these
Wooded Zacynthus: but itself it lies
A lowland, out beneath the dusking skies
Far off to westward, but the rest apart,
Facing the dawning and the sun's uprise.
Rough it is, but the lads it rears are brave;
And for my part naught sweeter might I crave
Than that same land of mine.'

Book VII, lines 577–580, Book IX, lines 19–28.

'Thence sailing forward, heavy at our heart,
To the Cyclopes' land we took our way:
A people proud, to whom no law is known;
And, trusting to the deathless gods alone,
They plant not and they plough not, but the earth
Bears all they need unfurrowed and unsown:
Barley and wheat, and vines whose mighty juice
Swells the rich clusters, when the rain of Zeus
Gives increase; and among that race are kept
No common councils nor are laws in use.
But on the high peaks and the hill-sides bare
In hollow caves they live, and each one there
To his own wife and children deals the law,
Neither has one of other any care.'

Book IX, lines 105–115.

Odysseus
and the Cyclops

Gustave Moreau

The World of Odysseus's Travels

Thence we sailed on, escaping glad from death,
Yet heart-sore for the comrades we had lost.

THIS REFRAIN RUNS THROUGH THE EARLY ADVENTURES OF ODYSSEUS on his return from Troy. At first Odysseus loses a few men, then a few ships. They sail on and meet ever more terrible dangers, as predicted by the witch Circe. Finally, the passage involving the oxen of the Sun, which was previewed as early as the prologue, results in the death of Odysseus's last companions, before he lands, alone and miserable, on the island of Calypso.

The journey begins on the coast of Thrace, in the land of the Ciconians, where Odysseus ventures a raid. Then a storm pushes his fleet due south, to Cape Maleia and Cythera. The north wind prevents Odysseus from sailing up the west coast of the Peloponnese, and sends him drifting for nine days. It is cloudy from then on, and landmarks are blurred. Their first landing, in the country of the Lotus-Eaters, was probably in Libya, or so the historian Herodotus thought. After this, the poet does not give enough information about sailing times and directions for us to reconstruct where they really went. In Ancient times, several adventures were located in Sicily: the Cyclopes and the Laestrygonians, also the island of the Sun and the monsters Charybdis and Scylla. The floating island of Aeolia was linked to the Lipari islands. According to the poet, Circe, on the other hand, lived on the side *where the sun rises*, or in the extreme east, in Colchis, which would have involved a magical voyage on the River of Ocean which is thought, in epic cosmography, to circle the inhabited earth and provide access to the Underworld. Phaeacia was often located in Corfu by the Ancients. In fact, Odysseus's voyage was very largely imaginary, and probably composite: it sometimes calls on other tales of voyages, such as that of the ship Argos which Jason sailed to Colchis in search of the Golden Fleece.

Apart from the gradual disappearance of Odysseus's companions, two relatively contradictory elements combine to give the story a certain unity. The first stems from the nature of the tests Odysseus must undergo: he must accept the human condition, and he must also not forget about returning home.

The Lotus Eaters

The Lotus-eaters; who against our crew
Devised not hurt, but gave them of the fruit
To taste upon the lotus-trees that grew.
But whoso of them once began to eat
The lotus-fruit, that is as honey sweet,
Had no will longer in him to return
Or bring back tidings, but desired to fleet
His days among the lotus-eating men,
Eating the lotus, nor return again.
Howbeit I drove them weeping to the ships,
And to the ships' holds haled and bound them then
Under the benches.

Book IX, lines 92–99.

The stay with the Lotus Eaters marks Odysseus's entry into the world of marvels. This second adventure is concerned with the danger of forgetting. What exactly is this hallucinogenic fruit? We do not know, but the essential image is of Odysseus not allowing his companions to find happiness in a far-off place, and reminding them of their duty to return home. This theme, which is valid both for Odysseus and for his companions, recurs in the stories recounted in the palace of Alcinous. It is true that the characters in *The Odyssey* are not alone in danger of forgetting Ithaca. The audiences of the poem, too, might have wanted to stay on the islands of the lotus people. *When you leave for Ithaca, / Hope that the way will be long …* wrote the Greek poet Cavafy. Perhaps Odysseus's admonitions were also addressed to the guests of the Phaeacian feast and, beyond that, to the reader: the pleasure of the stories is not timeless, we too must leave its enchanting world. Another thing which unites the stories told in the palace of Alcinous is their sense of adventure. *That of its folk I may inquire and know, / If they be fierce and lawless, men of blood, / Or hospitable and of godly mood.* This theme is repeated several times. In the opening lines of the poem, we are told that Odysseus had discovered many customs, or, to put it in a more traditional way, had got to learn the ways of many men. The voyages of Odysseus are investigations: he wants to learn, even at the risk of losing his life and not returning home. And this learning process is mainly concerned with the difference between savagery and civilisation.

The Cyclopes

The story of the man-eating giant and the hero who escapes from him by
blinding him in the eye can be found in many countries, from north Africa to
the Caucasus and in the Thousand and One Nights. Here the poet assumes
everyone knows the story, and does not even mention that Polyphemus has only
one eye. But the way he tells the story is individual to him. It begins with an
almost wholly negative description of the Cyclopes in general: they have no laws
and they do not work, they hold no meetings and they have no cities. Later, the
poet adds that they also do not have any boats. Their life is primeval, as in the
Golden Age, but the poet's main concern is to describe what they do not have
as a way of outlining his concept of humanity. Immediately afterwards, he
describes the island next to that of the Cyclopes through the eyes of an explorer
seeking to found a prosperous colony. Then Odysseus decides to go and take a
closer look at the people who inhabit the Cyclopes' land. We find the cave of
Polyphemus, that of a model shepherd, with lambs and goats all divided up by
age, cheeses set out neatly on racks, and milk standing ready to curdle. Homer
then returns to the theme of the social life that is missing, which is then pushed
to extremes through the monstrous behaviour of Polyphemus.

A cave upon the headland came in view,
High-vaulted, nigh the sea, with laurel trees
Shaded, and flocks about it not a few
Of sheep and goats lay sleeping, and around
Were reared great boulders sunk into the ground
To make a courtyard wall, filled up between
With tall-stemmed pines and oak trees lofty-crowned.
And there a giant man was wont to sleep,
Far and alone who shepherded his sheep,
Nor went among his fellows, choosing there
A lonely life in lawlessness to keep.
Mighty of frame he was, a monster dread,
Not like a man of them who live on bread,
But like some wooded crag that high aloft
Among the mountains rears its lonely head.

Book IX, lines 182–192.

The Death of Polyphemus, by Marc
Chagall (1887−1985). Homer
said nothing about where the
Cyclops's eye was located, and
painters had to invent their own
solutions, which varied even in
Antiquity, the episode being one
of the earliest to be illustrated,
from the 7th century BC.

Odysseus's Trick

Naturally, this social misfit has no idea about the laws of hospitality. He even laughs at Odysseus and the moral and religious rules which Zeus supervises for mankind. While the suitors devoured Odysseus's assets on Ithaca, now Polyphemus devours Odysseus's companions. The lion to which he is compared seems, for once, to be less savage and monstrous than he is.

So said I, and he answered not again
With ruthless heart, but leapt upon my men,
And at a single clutch a pair of them
Caught, and like puppies dashed them on his den,
So that their brains were spattered on the floor,
Wetting the earth; then limb from limb he tore,
And like a mountain lion supped on them
Devouring, and left nothing, less or more,
Entrails and flesh and marrowy bones.

Book IX, lines 287–293.

Faced with this savage, Odysseus uses his intelligence. The next day, while Polyphemus takes his sheep out to graze, our hero transforms one of the Cyclops's clubs into a sharp stake which, with the help of his crew, he can use to gouge out the monster's eye. When Polyphemus comes back, Odysseus offers him a cup of dark wine to send him to sleep; he has a further trick to play as well, which is also mentioned in other versions of the story.

'Cyclops, you ask the name men call me by:
That I will utter forth; and likewise you
Give me a guest-gift as you sware to do.
Noman my name is; Noman am I called
By them who bare me and by all my crew.
So said I; and he answered me straightway
With ruthless heart: Then Noman shall my prey
Be after all his fellows, and they first:
This gift I give you as my guest today.
These words he spake, and rolling backwards leant,
Lying along, his thick neck sideways bent:
For sleep that conquers all laid hold on him:
While from his gullet jets of wine there went,
And gobbets of man's flesh mixed therewithal
That in his drunken vomit he let fall.
Then in the embers piled I thrust the stake
To heat it, cheering on my fellows all,
That none might falter, but with courage good
Stand by: but when the stake of olive-wood
All through glowed fiercely, and began, though green,
To kindle, then amid the rest I stood,
And pulled it from the fire and bore it nigh,
While in our hearts a god breathed courage high.
Then the sharp-pointed stake of olive-wood
They took and thrust it deep into his eye.
And I leant hard above it, with a will
Twirling it round, as with a boring-drill
A man drills through the timbers of a ship
While two below him keep it running still,
Handling the strap both ways to make it go
Backward and forward swiftly: even so
The fiery-pointed stake we twirled, and round
Its heated end the blood began to flow.
And all his lids and brows were scorched and marred
In the fierce vapour, as the eyeball charred

And the nerves shrank and crackled in the fire;
As even when a blacksmith, to make hard
Broad axe or adze, in the cold water-flood
Dips it with hissing scream (for that makes good
The strength of iron), tempering it: so
His eye hissed round the stake of olive-wood.
Then from his lips a great and awful shout
Brake, that the rock-walls echoed round about,
And we in terror fled away, while he
The stake bespattered all with blood pulled out
With both his hands and cast it far away,
And called out loudly, wallowing where he lay,
For help to the Cyclopes who in caves
Dwelt on the wind-swept headlands round the bay.
Hearing him call, they came from far and nigh
And questioning him what ailed him, standing by
About the cave, and asked: What ails you so,
O Polyphemus, that aloud you cry,
To break our sleep, through the immortal night?
Is any mortal man in your despite
Driving away your flocks? is any man
Slaying yourself, by treachery or by might?
And mighty Polyphemus from the den
Answered: O friends, Noman it is of men
Slays me, by treachery nor by any might.
Then answered they with winged words again:
Now then if no man does you violence
And all alone you are, upon your sense
Some malady is come from Zeus on high,
Against the which there is no sure defence.
Then to your father, Lord Poseidon, pray
To heal you. So they said, and went their way.
But in my heart I laughed, because my name
And pure device had led him quite astray.

Book IX, lines 364–414.

At dawn, to escape from the cave, Odysseus ties himself and his companions beneath the stoutest rams in the flock, and so they escape without being noticed by the naive and from now on pitiful Cyclops: when his favourite ram goes out last and with an uncertain step (because it is carrying Odysseus under it), he thinks it is because the animal feels pity for his poor master. Odysseus then makes a mistake, one that will cost him dear, revealing out of pure boastfulness his real name before he sails away, which allows Polyphemus to denounce him to his father, Poseidon.

In this episode, Odysseus's trick in the face of the Cyclopes' strength is supported by a pun in the Greek language. In some contexts, the name that Odysseus gives himself, 'Noman', is almost exactly the same as a Greek word meaning 'intelligence, cunning'. The word also appears in Greek in one of the epithets attached to the name of the hero, 'the ingenious one'. Thus at the same time Odysseus conceals his identity while revealing his nature.

The Island of Aeolia

After escaping from the Cyclopes, Odysseus and his companions arrive at the floating island of the king of the winds, Aeolus, who welcomes them warmly and gives Odysseus a present, a goatskin (containing all the winds, so that the breeze will push their ships towards Ithaca; but he does not explain what is in the skin). Odysseus's companions are both jealous and curious, and open it as soon as Odysseus is asleep, which unleashes a storm just when Ithaca is in sight.

Odysseus beneath the ram (black-figured oil flask from the end of the 6th century BC). The motif of Odysseus's escape with his companions is well represented in black-figured ceramics. Odysseus is sometimes shown alone, and sometimes he manages to brandish his spear while still tied to the ram!

The Laestrygonians attack
Odysseus's boat (Roman fresco).

The Laestrygonians

When they return, Aeolus angrily sends them away, thinking they must be devils, and their voyage meanders once more towards unknown countries where, mysteriously, *so near do night and day their pathways keep*, and where the inhabitants are gigantic cannibals even more fearsome than the Cyclopes, despite their much more civilised appearance.

... the mighty Laestrygons
In crowds innumerable sallied out,
Like giants, not like mortal men to view;
And from the cliff's edge mighty rocks they threw,
Then awful was the noise that rose at once
From ships they splintered, and from men they slew.
And spearing them like fishes where they lay
They bore them for their loathly meal away.

Book X, lines 119–124.

The only boat in the whole fleet to escape the carnage is that of Odysseus, which he had taken the precaution of mooring outside the Laestrygons' harbour, Once more the refrain is repeated:

Thence we sailed onward, joyful to have fled
With life, but for our fellows perished
Grieving at heart.

And they in a wide clearing in a glen
Found Circe's palace, built of polished stone,
And round it no man was, but beasts alone,
Hill-wolves and lions, over whom the witch
With evil drugs had her enchantment thrown.
Nor sprang they at the men, but round them they
Ramped fawning with their outstretched tails asway,
Even as when the master from a meal
Rises, his dogs about him fawning play:
For thence his wont is some scraps to bring
To appease their maw: so round them in a ring
Fawned then the lions and the strong-clawed wolves;
While they in terror saw so strange a thing.
And now upon the fair-tressed goddess's floor
They stood, and from her porches through the door
Heard Circe singing sweetly, as within
She wrought, the deathless high-built loom before,
As works of goddesses are wont to be,
A web thin, lovely, wonderful to see.
Then silence brake Polites, prince of men,
Most lief and dear of all my crew to me:
Lo, friends, within, before the loom built high,
A goddess or a woman, who thereby
Sings sweetly, that around her all the floor
Echoes: now make we haste on her to cry.
So said he: and they called aloud and cried;
Then issuing forth she straight threw open wide
The shining doors and called them; and they all
Went in their folly trooping at her side.
Only Eurylochus held back: for he
suspected in his heart some treachery.

Book X, lines 210–232.

Circe the Magician

A Magician

She led them in and set them down arow
And mixed with Pramnian wine, their drink to be,
Cheese and pale honey and barley-flour withal,
But in the flour a baleful drug let fall
To make them quite forget their native land,
And gave it, and they took and drank it all.
Then straight she smote them with the wand she bore,
And penned them in the sties; and now they wore
The heads and voice and bristled body of swine
But kept their senses perfect as before.
Thus weeping they were pent, and at their feet
Circe threw nuts and acorns for their meat
And berries of the dogwood, such as swine
That sleep upon the ground are wont to eat.

Book X, lines 233–243.

MAGIC HAS VERY LITTLE PLACE IN *THE ILIAD* AND *THE ODYSSEY*, and seems even to be deliberately avoided. This is the only instance of men being transformed into animals. The narrator takes care to warn his audience of the dangers facing Odysseus's companions, which serves once more to heighten their naivety and stupidity, even if one of them behaves more prudently.

Odysseus is informed by Eurylochus and wants to save his companions. On the way he is helped by Hermes who gives him an antidote, the black and white plant that the gods call *moly*, and explains in detail what he has to do. The drug enables him to be touched by the magic wand but not harmed. Circe then collapses, and becomes a welcoming and hospitable woman. She washes Odysseus, turns his companions back into humans, invites the hero to sleep with her, and they all finish the year in her palace, until, strangely enough, it is Odysseus's companions who remind him of the need to return home. Circe then tells them they will have to pass through Hades to hear the prophecies of the divine Tiresias.

So said she: but I inly for a space
Mused and was full of longing to embrace
The ghost of my dead mother. Thrice I sprang
Towards her, fain to clasp her face to face;
And thrice from out my hands to clasp her spread
Like to a shadow or a dream she fled.
And grief waxed ever keener at my heart,
And winged words I spake to her and said:
My mother, wherefore draw thou thus aside
From me and will not my embrace abide,
That we in this dark realm may cast our hands
Each round the other, and be satisfied
With frozen wailing? or should this have been
A phantom only that the awful Queen
Persephone has sent me, to the end
My grief and sorrow may be yet more keen?
So spake I; and the Queen my mother so
Made answer: O my child, foredoomed to woe
Beyond all mortal men, Persephone
God's daughter mocks you with no lying show:
But in this wise it is when men are dead:
From flesh and bones the strength is minished;
But these the strong might of the burning fire
Consumes, when once the spirit forth is fled
From the white bones.

Book XI, lines 204–222.

Hades

Odysseus and His Mother

THE DESCENT TO HADES ELEVATES ODYSSEUS TO THE RANK OF A HERO SUCH AS ORPHEUS, Heracles and Theseus. But the poet does not at all stress the difficulties of the journey. It is less of a test than a new and pathetic experience of the human condition. After death, the poor life that the 'souls' of the dead live is pitiful. It is not, as in the myth where Orpheus is searching for Eurydice, and cannot embrace her because he turns round, but because death introduces an irreparable break. Even the words they exchange only make this void deeper.

Odysseus and Achilles

Odysseus has many encounters in Hades, and this Book has probably attracted more additions than most in the course of time. He learns from Tiresias the future stages of his wanderings. He sees noble ladies and great criminals. He talks to the main heroes of the Trojan war who are dead: Agamemnon, Ajax and Achilles, which once again demonstrates his superiority over them. Thus the dominion which Achilles, the hero of *The Iliad*, exercises over the dead, about which Odysseus compliments him courteously, is, in his own eyes, no more than a kind of masquerade. This emphasises the superiority of Odysseus's choice, which is survival, over that of Achilles, which is death.

'Speak not soft words concerning death to me,
Glorious Odysseus: rather had I be
A thrall upon the acres to a man
Portionless and sunk low in poverty,
Than over all the perished dead below
Hold lordship.'

Book XI, lines 488–491.

And all the while the ship well-builded drew
Anigh the island where the Sirens are;
For swift before the steady wind it flew.
Then the breeze dropped at once, and windless lay
A calm about us, and the waves at play
God lulled to rest. [...]
While I cut a great round cake of wax
And in my fingers wrought it busily.
And soon the wax began to melt and run [...]
With it I stopped the ears of every one.
Then foot and hand with cables from the mast
Standing upright aboard they bound me fast
In the mast-socket, and themselves sat down
And the grey water with the oars upcast.
Now when at hailing distance we came by
Skimming the sea, they failed not to espy
The swift sea-travelling ship as near it drew,
And with a shrill sweet voice began to cry:
'Come hither, come, Odysseus far-renowned,
High fame of the Achaeans, lay aground
Your ship that you may listen to our voice:
For never yet has mariner been found
That past our shore in his black ship would go,
Nor hear the sweet songs from our lips that flow
And hence a gladder and a wiser man
Pass on his voyage: for the tale we know
Of all the Argive and the Trojan toil
When in wide Troy the gods' will bred them broil,
And whatsoever things have come to pass
We know, upon the earth's all-nurturing soil ...'

Book XII, lines 166-191.

The Island
of the Sirens

So sang they sweetly; and with yearning strong
I fain had listened to their lovely song,
And with bent brows I beckoned to my men
To set me free: but they rowed hard along.
And Perimedes rising from his oar
Came with Eurylochus, and bonds yet more
Drew round me and yet harder tied me down,
Until they had rowed past that magic shore.
And when the Sirens' voice and melody
Passed out of hearing, they immediately
The wax that I had stopped their ears withal
Took out, and from my bonds unfastened me.

Book XII, lines 192–200.

PREVIOUS PAGES
The Sirens, by Christopher Wood
(1901–1960). In this strange,
bewitching painting, the Sirens
seem to be winning, helped by
Poseidon (though he does not
appear in this part of Homer's
story).

OPPOSITE
Odysseus and the Sirens (detail
from a red-figured stamnos,
c 475 BC). The image of
Odysseus bound to the mast
but wanting to go to the Sirens
often inspired painters in
Ancient Greece. But in Homer
the Sirens are only voices, or
more precisely two voices
singing together.

OVERLEAF
Odysseus between Scylla and Charybdis,
by Henry Fuseli (1741–1825).
Fuseli rightly focused on the
contrast between Odysseus's
human armour, with his
ridiculous shield (in the poem,
Odysseus even takes hold of 'two
great lances') and the monstrous
power of the fantastic beings.

IN ANTIQUITY, THE SIRENS WERE NOT THE SEA-DWELLING FISH-WOMEN that we have known since the Middle Ages, but bird-women who perched on rocks. This explains why they are associated here with singing and epic poetry. The way Odysseus prepares to meet them, following all Circe's recommendations, is very strange. Once again, he is set apart from his companions, but this time he is the one who is tempted and wants to forget about returning home, which means he would die (the fate awaiting anyone who visits the Sirens), while his companions obey orders and, with their ears stopped with beeswax, reinforce the bonds holding Odysseus down. Thus the hero makes himself available to the bird-women, but remains fixed to the mast, which symbolises the return home.

This episode has given rise to many allegorical interpretations. It has been seen as man's struggle against pleasure. The wonderful songs of the Sirens treat the same subject as the epics, particularly *The Iliad*, namely the Trojan war. In addition, the Sirens attract Odysseus by referring to his presence in *The Iliad*. This makes the episode seem like a new story within a story which repeats the poetry and values of *The Iliad*. The epic is both magnified as an unsurpassable achievement and cast out to a deadly hinterland.

The Sirens promise Odysseus a song that will make him happy. But if any mortal does stop to listen, he will die, which makes the song something deeply inhuman. Homer uses the Sirens as a dramatic version of the Muses.

But while in dread of doom our gaze we bent
Upon the whirlpool, Scylla swooped and rent
Six of my comrades from the hollow ship
That were for might of hand most excellent.
And to the swift ship turning back my eye
I saw their feet and hands caught up on high,
While for the last time upon me they called
And my name uttered with their dying cry.
As when upon a jutting point of land
With his long rod a fisher takes his stand
And strewing ground-bait for the lesser fish
Darts into the sea-water from his hand
The wild-ox horn that tips his lance, and each
He strikes is flung out gasping on the beach;
So gasping they were dragged against the rock
Up where the fiend devoured them out of reach,
Screaming aloud and stretching out to me
Their helpless hands in awful agony.
Most piteous was that sight of all I bore
While I explored the pathways of the sea.

Book XII, lines 244–259.

The Final Tests

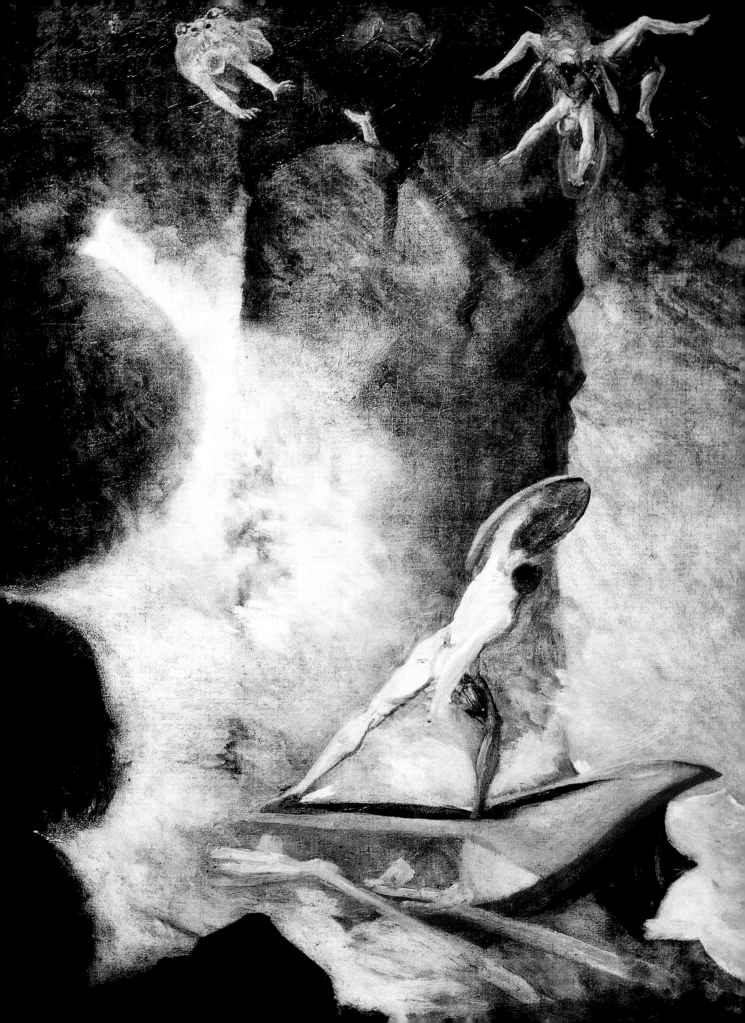

Hermes steals Apollo's oxen (detail from a hydria, or water jar). Only a cunning young god like Hermes can steal Apollo's oxen without being punished. This is an episode from Hymns, said to be by Homer (which form a body of very interesting epic verse, often underrated).

Charybdis and Scylla

THE SIRENS ARE IMMEDIATELY FOLLOWED BY TWO MONSTERS who send the story deeper still into the world of fantasy. To begin with, despite the warnings of Circe, Odysseus wants to take on Scylla as he fought opponents in *The Iliad*, with armour and lance. But, the poet insists, *The Odyssey* is not *The Iliad*, and glory cannot be achieved in this way. The hero, his eyes fixed on Charybdis in her terrifying pool, does not even see Scylla seize his companions.

Odysseus will meet Charybdis again, after losing his companions, and only just escapes death. Before that comes the last test, the one announced in the first lines of the poem, describing the fatal mistake made by Odysseus's companions and their punishment.

The Oxen of the Sun

The island of the Sun god is inhabited by sacred flocks, as were to be found in many regions of Ancient Greece. Here, the animals seem to have been left to themselves, as though they were wild. Odysseus had been warned of the sacrilege his companions were in danger of committing, and had tried not to put in at the island. Unable to avoid doing so, he had made them swear not to touch the gods' animals. But, once more taking advantage of Odysseus falling asleep, they went off hunting, killed many oxen and prepared to sacrifice them so they could eat them. The hunt is mixed in with the sacrifice in an unusual way, and the betrayal of the oath compounds the men's sacrilege. Such a ritual cannot be accepted by the gods.

The gods wrought miracles that pass men's wit:
The flayed hides crawled, and round about the spit
The roast flesh and the raw began to low,
And voices as of oxen came from it.

Book XII, lines 394–396.

The fools did not understand, and feasted for six days. Their punishment struck them as soon as they put to sea again. Odysseus alone survived.

The Last Storm

A storm closed the story in the palace of Alcinous, just as a storm had preceded
Odysseus's arival in Phaeacia. The fickleness of the sea haunted the Greeks in
the Archaic period. In *Works and Days*, the poet Hesiod viewed sea voyages as a
dangerous last resort and, unlike the solid values of earth and work, the sea was
for a long time associated with risk, savagery and people losing their way. But
storms were very useful to the poet, who could use them to link episodes as
he pleased, and have them reverberate through the story.

And a sharp gust snapped either forward stay
That held the mast up, and it fell away
Aft, carrying all the yards and rigging down,
That in a heap along the hold they lay;
And on the after-deck the steersman's head
It struck, and smashed the bones and laid him dead,
And like a diver from the deck he fell,
As from his bones the valiant spirit fled.
Then in one moment out of heaven there came
A crash of thunder and a sheet of flame:
And the ship, smitten by the bolt of God,
Staggered from stem to stern through all her frame,
And filled with sulphurous vapour, and therefrom
The crew fell off, and on the billowing foam
Round the black ship like seafowl ere they sank
Went drifting: thus God stayed their journey home.
But up and down the ship I paced alone
Till all the planking of the sides was gone,
Wrenched from the keel that naked on the wave,
With the mast broken from it, floated on.
Yet on the mast one after-stay held fast,
Made of ox-hide; with it I lashed the mast
And keel together, and on them I clung
Drifting along before the bitter blast.

Book XII, lines 409–425.

Neptune Calming the Storm, by Peter Paul
Rubens (1577–1640). In *The Odyssey*
it is Poseidon (Neptune in Latin) who
unleashes storms, while here it is Zeus
himself who is taking the initiative.

OVERLEAF
The massacre of the suitors (detail from a
red-figured bell krater by the painter from
Ixion, c. 330 BC).

The Final Tests   207

The Reconquest _{of} Ithaca

ODYSSEUS RETURNS TO ITHACA IN CAREFULLY MANAGES STAGES.
HIS FAITHFUL SERVANT EUMAEUS WELCOMES HIM BUT DOES NOT
RECOGNISE HIM. WHEN TELEMACHUS ARRIVES IN THE
SWINEHERD'S HUT, ODYSSEUS REVEALS HIMSELF TO HIS SON.
THEN, TO GET INTO HIS PALACE INCOGNITO, HE DISGUISES
HIMSELF AS A BEGGAR, UNTIL THE DAY HE TAKES HIS REVENGE.

'Artful indeed and subtle would he be
Who, meeting you, in any sort of guile
Outdid you, even though a god were he.
Hardy of heart, insatiate of deceit,
Full of devices! so you thought not meet
Even in your own land to lay aside
Your treacheries and your words that love to cheat.
But now no longer let us talk thereof,
Being both well practised in the craft we love:
Since you in counsel and in tale-telling
Are far away all mortal me above:
Even as I all gods in fame excel
Of craft and wisdom. Yet you knew not well
Pallas Athene now, the maid of Zeus,
Who stand beside you danger to repel
In all your labours, and have made you dear
In sight of all Phaeacia, and appear
Now once again beside you to devise
Counsel with you and hide this treasure here
That at your going, by my art and thought,
The lordly people of Phaeacia brought.

Book XIII, lines 291–305.

With Eumaeus
the Swineherd

At once the baying hounds espying him
Gave tongue and ran at him with evil will.
But down Odysseus in his subtlety
Crouched, and let fall his staff: and there has he
By his own steading in unseemly wise
Been mangled; but the swineherd hastily
Sprang up, and from his hand the hide let fall
And ran swift-footed by the forecourt wall,
Chiding his hounds, and putting them to flight
With stones, and to his master spake withal:
'O aged man, full little to your bane
There lacked, by these my hounds pulled down and slain;
Whence shame had covered me, beyond all else
The gods have given me of distress and pain.
Since for my godlike master, sitting here,
In lamentable wise I mourn, and rear
The fatted hogs for other men to eat,
While he for lack of food makes evil cheer
In alien lands and cities far away,
If yet he lives and sees the light of day.
But follow me, old man, into the hut
That you with bread and wine your heart may stay.
Thereafter shall you tell me, as is meet,
Whence you have come, and all the tale repeat
Of your distress.'

So saying, the swineherd good
Let him indoors and set him on a seat;
Heaping a couch beneath him therewithin
Of brushwood, and a wild goat's shaggy skin
Thick-haired and large, his own bed's covering.
Glad was Odysseus welcome thus to win;
And spake a word and uttered: 'Now may still
Zeus and the other deathless gods fulfil,
O friend, the utmost of your heart's desire,
For that you give me welcome with good will.'
And answering spake you, herder of the swine,
Eumaeus: 'Nay, my friend, the wrong were mine
To scorn a stranger, were he worse than you.
Strangers and beggars are in care divine.
How small soe'er, the grace to these we show
Is precious. But with bondsmen is it so
That always they have dread of mastery
When to young masters they their service owe.
Sure by the gods cut off from home is he
Who well had loved me [...]
Wherefore my master had an ampler wage
Given me, if here he had attained old age.
But he is perished.'

Book XIV, lines 29–58, 67–68.

Odysseus in the Piggery

ON THE ORDERS OF ALCINOUS, the Phaeacians brought Odysseus to Ithaca by night
in a magical voyage, while he slept. He wakes up not knowing where he has
been left. In the cave where the Phaeacians left Odysseus, Athene, disguised as
a shepherd, tells the hero that he is in Ithaca. Immediately, he hides his identity
and invents a story. Athene then reveals herself to Odysseus. This bout of
trickery sets the mood for the decisive tests which must be passed. Odysseus
must hide, observe and suffer.

> 'Ane tell you all the troubles you are yet
> Fated to bear within your house well-wrought.
> Yet notwithstanding must your heart be strong,
> And tell no man nor woman that from long
> Wandering you come, but many sorrows yet
> Endure in silence, and abide men's wrong.'
>
> Book XIII, lines 306–310.

Now Athene turns Odysseus into a hideous beggar and advises him to go first
near the raven's cliff to see the only servant who has remained faithful to him,
Eumaeus, while she goes to Sparta to fetch Telemachus.
Then the simple swineherd gives a fine lesson in hospitality, despite his
poverty: bread and wine, and a goatskin. Eumaeus explains the situation at the
palace to Odysseus and tells him that Telemachus has gone away. Odysseus
pretends he is a wandering Cretan, returning from Troy via Egypt. In this
second false tale, the only truth is that Odysseus is alive, but this is the only
thing that Eumaeus cannot believe. The following day, the swineherd in turn
tells his story, how he was the son of a king but had become a slave. There is
nothing fantastic about such tales, they simply tell of the misfortunes of real
life in the Mediterranean with its pirates, storms and harbours or refuges.
In Sparta, Athene hastens the departure of Telemachus, helping him to avoid
being ambushed by the suitors. When he reaches Ithaca, the young hero goes
immediately to Eumaeus.

PREVIOUS PAGES
The Return of Odysseus, by Giorgio de
Chirico (1888–1978). Perhaps
Chirico knew the interpretation
which sees Odysseus's return to
Ithaca as the first victory of bourgeois
conformism. In this picture, painted
at the end of his life, there is humour
and derision, but we are far from
his moving *Hector and Andromache*
(see p. 51).

ABOVE
*Minerva Telling Ulysses that he Must Present
Himself at Court*, by Orazio Sanacchini
(1532–1577).

With Eumaeus the Swineherd   **217**

Telemachus in the House of Eumaeus

And round Telemachus as he drew nigh
The hounds deep-baying came, and gave no cry,
But fawned about him; and Odysseus bright
Took note, and heard the tramp of feet thereby. [...]
Not fully spoken was the word,
When his own son stood in the portico.
Up then the swineherd starting in surprise
The cups, wherein he mixed in careful wise
The flame-bright wine, let fall, and to the prince
Ran up and kissed his head and lovely eyes,
And both his hands; and down the big tear fell.
And as a father, who his son loves well,
Embraces him as when from a foreign land
In the tenth year he comes at home to dwell;
His only one and well-beloved, for whom
Much he has wrought in sorrow and in gloom:
So the bright swineherd clasped and kissed the prince
Telemachus as one escaped from doom.

Book XVI, lines 4–6, 11–21.

Since Odysseus is unable to reveal his identity, it is for Telemachus to act: he sends
Eumaeus to warn Penelope, and her alone, of his return, and advises the supposed
beggar not to go into town, as he could not, he regretted, guarantee his safety.
Once Eumaeus has gone, Odysseus and Telemachus can be reunited, once Athene
has given the hero his noble appearance once more. Telemachus explains about the
suitors. The plan they develop together involves Odysseus remaining secret about
his return and taking on the appearance of a *pitiful beggar* to enter the palace with
Eumaeus, but without Telemachus who will go on ahead of them. They must put
up with all the outrages until, at a sign from Odysseus, Telemachus will hide all
the weapons in the great hall, except those of the father and the son.

The Threats of the Goatherd

Eumaeus and Odysseus set off for the town. Arriving by the fountain, they meet
the goatherd Melanthius, an unfaithful servant who is taking his finest animals to
the suitors, and who now badly insults Eumaeus.

'Now look you, surely here
A rascal leads a rascal: even so
Like by the side of like god makes to go.
O wretched swineherd, whither lead you now
This hog, this beggar-man, to bring us woe,
This canker of the feast. [...]
Give him to me to keep the cotes from harm,
To sweep the stalls and carry on his arm
Green branches for the kids, and drinking whey
Wax to a stout-thighed labourer on the farm.
But all his knowledge is of doing ill,
Nor will he set to work with a good will,
But rather choose to shamble through the town
Begging for food his greedy guts to fill.
Yet this I tell you, and it shall be so,
If to divine Odysseus's house he go,
Bruised ribs a many will await him there
From stools that men about his head will throw.'
He spoke, and in his folly lifting high
His heel, upon the swine as he went by
Kicked him, but from the pathway thrust him not:
Steadfast he stood, debating inwardly
With one blow of his staff to smite him dead
Or grapple with him and dash down his head,
Lifting him off his feet, upon the ground;
Yet he refrained, and nought he did nor said.
But with reproachful words and visage grim
The herder of the swine brake out on him.

Book XVII, lines 217–220, 223–239.

A dog that lay near by lift up his head
And pricked his ears: Odysseus's hound was he,
Argus, whom that man much-enduring bred;
But got no profit from his rearing ere
To holy Troy he overseas must fare;
So time agone the young man took him out
To hunt the pricket or wild goat or hare:
But now, his master being far astray,
Before the gate thrust out of doors he lay
Upon a dunghill where the dung of mules
And oxen was heaped up to take away
To the great field that was Odysseus's plot,
That there the thralls might spread it out to rot.
There the dog Argus full of vermin lay;
Yet then to know his master failed he not;
And wagged his tail and both his ears laid low,
But nearer to his lord he could not go.
And he turned sidelong to wipe off a tear
Privily, that Eumaeus did not know:
And thus inquired: 'Eumaeus, to mine eyes
This hound that here upon the dunghill lies
Is goodly-shaped and marvellous to see:
But I would be assured of my surmise,
If as in beauty he excelled in speed,
Or was but such a plaything as men breed
For show, and princes keep for luxury
Beside them at the table where they feed.'
And answering spake you, herder of the swine,
Eumaeus: 'This indeed as you divine
Was the man's hound who far away has died ...

Odysseus Begs
in His Palace

Had but his limbs and deeds not known decline
From what he was of old when Troyward-bound
Odysseus left him, you would be astound
To see his strength and speed: no beast of chase
Escaped him in the tangled woodland ground;
And he excelled in hunting of the slot;
But now has fallen on him an evil lot:
His master from the land is far away,
Dead, and the careless women tend him not.'
But black death fell on Argus, having seen
Odysseus after twenty years were gone.

Book XVII, lines 291–319, 326–327.

The Faithful Dog

IN EPICS, DOGS AROUSE FEAR MORE THAN AFFECTION. If we are to believe the opening lines of *The Iliad*, they devour corpses. Priam, imagining Troy in ruins, is afraid that his own dogs might attack his corpse. The suitors threaten Eumaeus, whose dogs are fearsome, with the same fate. Shameless people are called 'dogs' or 'bitches'. However, unlike the wolf, the dog is seen as close to man and faithful. This applies not only to thoroughbred dogs, whose beauty brings credit to their masters and which are represented on vases of the Archaic period, but mainly to dogs associated with aristocratic hunts, which are just as clever as their masters at tracking game. Argus (meaning 'Dazzler'), the only dog in an epic to have a name, is a model for all dogs. He combines his speed with strength and cunning, the qualities of his master. The pathos of the scene stems partly from the fact that he has lost these powers: he is too old and has not been cared for. He seems to symbolise the past, the misdeeds of the suitors and the impossibility of going back in time. But he recognises Odysseus: he is the first, and the only one, to recognise him without divine intervention. He is the one who authenticates Odysseus as Odysseus. His flair recreates the bond between the past and the present without, for the time being, anyone except Odysseus noticing.

When Odysseus takes off his rags to confront Irus, the palace's resident beggar, his muscular body astounds everybody, but no-one guesses the truth.

The Beggars' Fight

...Out into mid-floor
They pulled him, and the twain took guard; and now
Long-suffering bright Odysseus pondered sore
Whether to fell him dead with one great blow,
Or strike no harder than to lay him low:
And best be deemed, considering it, to hit
Lightly, that the Achaeans might not know.
Then the two stood on guard; and Irus hit
At the right shoulder, but Odysseus lit
Full upon Irus's neck below the ear,
So strongly that the bones were split.
And from his mouth the red blood straightway gushed,
As he lay rolled and gasping in the dust,
And his teeth clashed together as he fell,
And with his feet against the ground he thrust.
Then holding up their hands, into a shout
Of laughter broke the princely suitors out.

Book XVIII, lines 89–100.

Odysseus's success earns him praise and a place at one of the tables. But in fact, as the final image of the suitors roaring with laughter reveals, and as Telemachus says a little later, this fight heralds a much more serious one, and a much more glorious triumph.

Then Penelope comes downstairs wearing her veil to reprimand her son for the poor welcome given to the beggar, and to charm the suitors. They fall immediately beneath her spell and produce little presents, hoping finally to win her hand. In the evening, when the suitors have left, Telemachus removes the weapons from the room, and Penelope comes down again to question her guest who, it seems, knew Odysseus well. Odysseus again pretends to be a Cretan, who had welcomed Odysseus and his companions to his palace very recently.

OVERLEAF
The Fight Between Odysseus and the Beggar, by Lovis Corinth (1858–1925). The parody in Corinth's treatment is not inappropriate: compared with the terrible fights at the Games in honour of Patroclus, the scrap with Irus has its comic aspects, Odysseus being by far the better fighter.

The Tears of Penelope

So told he many falsehoods seeming true,
And as she listened her tears poured anew
And her face melted, as on mountain peaks
Snow that descended when the west wind blew
Melts in the east, and with its melting, flow
Brim-full the swollen rivers; even so
Melted her lovely cheeks with tears for him
Who sat beside her, and she did not know.
But on his wife lamenting in such wise
Odysseus had compassion, yet his eyes
Like horn or iron kept behind the lids
Unwavering, and forbade the tears to rise.

Book XIX, lines 203–212.

Penelope is to be the last to recognise Odysseus and will be excluded from his
revenge. The poet delays this moment as long as possible, for it is the real end of
the epic. The closeness of the couple, which the queen does not acknowledge,
although Odysseus feels it keenly, is nevertheless perceptible and pathetic.

Eurycleia Recognises Odysseus

Odysseus tries to bring hope to Penelope without giving himself away, and, in
return for his kind words, the queen orders that he shall be looked after well. The
hero declines the offer of a bed to sleep in; he only requests one thing: that an
old servant washes his feet. Penelope agrees, and orders the nurse Eurycleia to do
this. Immediately, the old woman is struck by the resemblance betwen the beggar
and Odysseus. From then on, Odysseus is fearful of being recognised, particularly
since she knows about the scar on his foot.

Odysseus Is Recognised by his Nurse Eurycleia,
by Gustave Boulanger (1824–1888).

Sketch for *Odysseus Recognised by His Nurse Eurycleia*. Gustave Moreau's sketches are often, in our view, more expressive than his finished or incomplete canvases.

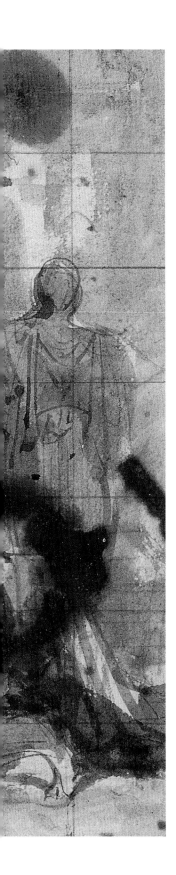

This the old woman, when she held the limb
Between her palms and felt it, rubbing him,
Knew, and let go his leg, and in the bath
It fell with clatter of the brazen rim;
And the bath tilted overthwart, and lay
Spilling the water: and at once dismay
And gladness seized her, and her eyes with tears
Filled up, and her voice could not find its way.
Then to Odysseus's chin her hand she set,
And cried: 'Odysseus's self you are, and yet
I knew you not, O nursling well-beloved,
Before my hands about my king had met.'

Book XIX, lines 467–479.

The hero of the tales returns to his country after his tests, but incognito, to have his exploits recognised. The marks on his body now often play an important part in his identification. Here, he interrupts the nurse's recognition immediately, to keep up the suspense and the feeling of agony: *'hold your peace, / Lest any other in the house may learn!'*. The fact that the nurse recognises the scar takes us back to Odysseus's childhood, and now we learn much more about the hero.

Odysseus was in fact wounded while hunting a wild boar with his grandfather, Autolycus, Penelope's father. Eurycleia, remembering this, also recalls the time when, long before, Autolycus chose the name Odysseus when the child was born. The grandfather's name, moreover, means 'True Wolf', and is accompanied by a subtitle that could not be more explicit: *master of thefts and perjuries*. This is a double negative of what Odysseus will be. The tricks of Odysseus and Penelope are inherited, but have served a rightful cause. In addition, Autolycus chose the name Odysseus for his grandson because he was full of hatred and anger at the time (in Greek *odyssasthai*). Odysseus, or The Quarreller, has the anger in his name which drives him to take on the suitors, and the anger of Poseidon, which cost him his misfortunes, and also that of his son, when he rebelled at the beginning of the poem.

Odysseus Plans His Revenge

From this point onward, Eurycleia will help in the preparations for Odysseus's revenge, which he thinks over during the night, while he observes his unfaithful servant women, *Laughing and making merry each with each*, leave the palace to sleep with the suitors. He curses his heart and tells it to be patient, as he was in the Cyclops's cave, waiting to attack it.

> Even as a pudding stuffed with fat and blood
> That on a glowing fire of kindled wood
> Hither and thither a man turns about,
> Fain that the roasting quickly be made good,
> So restlessly from side to side he tossed
> Revolving what device might help him most
> Upon the shameless suitors to lay hands,
> Being a single man against a host.

Book XX, lines 25–30.

Homer's psychology is often difficult to understand. The heart, the soul and the spirit are autonomous forces within the body, located in the guts, the belly and the chest.

This could be seen as the first description of a soul in conflict, something that will later torment authors of tragedies and philosophers. Plato, in his *Republic*, divides the soul into three parts: reason, anger (or courage, the two words being the same in Greek) and desire. He defines the just soul as one in which anger obeys reason and desire remains silent. In this passage, too, the choice of the men and women who give themselves up to pleasure is condemned, and Odysseus embodies a man's victory over sudden rage. It is because of such moments that the texts of the epics have been used for centuries as a model of moral instruction.

In fact, revenge is unleashed as the consequence of Penelope's idea, which Odysseus approves, to hold an archery contest the next day, the feast day of the god Apollo. When the suitors come back, they settle down in the great hall, fall to feasting once more, scorning Odysseus again, and ordering Telemachus to find a husband for his mother. His reaction sends them into hysterical laughter, a loss of control which prefigures the disaster about to befall them:

PREVIOUS PAGES
The Return of Odysseus, by William Patrick Roberts (1895–1980). The artist magnificently conveys the whirling *hubris* ('extravagance, violence') of the suitors, which seems to threaten even their shadows in this Vorticist painting, an English style developed before the First World War, combining Cubism and Futurism.

OPPOSITE
Odysseus, by Giacomo Manzu (1908–1991).

But subtle-souled Odysseus, now that he
Had balanced the great bow carefully
Looked it all over, even as a man
In viol-playing skilled and minstrelsy
Easily stretches round a new-cut pin
The string of twisted sheep-gut, fastened in
At either end, so then Odysseus bent
The mighty bow and took no pains therein:
And with his right hand plucked the string to try;
And it rang sweetly, like a swallow's cry,
And all the suitors' flesh upon them crept
And pain within them waxed exceedingly.
And giving token from the firmament
Zeus thundered loudly: but then well-content
Was patient bright Odysseus, for he knew
Deep-minded Cronus's son that sign had sent.
Then lifted he one arrow swift to haste
That on the table by him lay uncased –
But in the hollowed quiver lay the rest,
That the Achaeans shortly were to taste –
And laid it on the bridge as though no care
He took, and seated still upon his chair
Drew back the notch and bowstring and took aim,
And loosed the arrow straight before him there.
And of the row of axes missed he none
At the shaft's head, but through them every one,
And out, the heavy bronze-topped arrow went.

Book XXI, lines 404–423.

The Bow Test

THE EXACT NATURE OF THE TEST suggested by Penelope has been much discussed: how was it possible to make an arrow pass through the heads of twelve axes lined up in the courtyard? One thing is certain: Odysseus's great bow, which Penelope went to fetch from the palace treasury with such emotion, was not a simple one-piece bow, as was used in battle. It was a ceremonial bow of the composite type, used for special occasions, which bent inward when it was not being stretched, and was much more powerful but also much more difficult to handle. The first test was to bend it, the second to aim straight.

Skill in the use of a special bow was something many heroes shared, in Greek mythology and elsewhere. It was also a rite of access to royalty found in the Indo-Iranian world since the second millennium BC, in a sacred hymn of the *Rig–Veda*: 'I take the bow from the hands of the dead man for our domination, our prestige, our bravery.' The poet makes the test happen on the feast day of the supreme archer-god, Apollo, on the occasion of the new moon which begins the new year, twenty years after the beginning of the Trojan war. It was truly the decisive test.

The scene is built up with a great sense of dramatic tension. Telemachus tries first, but fails three times, perhaps because Odysseus shook his head. Then the suitors take the test: none of them can even bend the bow. Their two leaders are left, Antinous and Eurymachus. This is the moment Odysseus chooses, in secret, to reveal his identity to Eumaeus and the herdsman, so they will be ready to bolt the hall door at a signal from their master. Eurymachus heats the bow in vain, he too cannot bend it. Antinous tries to get out of trying, but Odysseus then claims his right to try his luck. Penelope pleads for him, saying that in his case there is of course no question of marriage or royalty; she will simply give him a few presents. Telemachus then sends his mother back to her room, where Athene plunges her into a deep sleep, and hands the bow to the beggar.

But subtle-souled Odysseus stripped away
From off him his disguise of mean array,
And leapt upon the mighty doorway-sill
Holding the bow and all the shafts that lay
Stored in the quiver, and before his feet
Poured out upon the floor the arrows fleet,
And there among the suitors cried aloud:
'Lo, this decisive trial is complete:
But now another target I descry,
That no man yet has hit; and I will try
If I may touch it, and Apollo give
Once more the glory to my archery.'
He spoke, and on Antinous laid the grim
Arrow: who then was lifting up to him
A fair two-handled golden cup to drink
Wine therefrom, and his hands were round the rim.
And death was from his mind a far-off thing;
For who could deem that mid men banqueting
One among many, mighty though he were,
Black weird on him and evil death might bring?
But aiming at his throat Odysseus drew
And loosed: and straight the arrow-point went through
His delicate neck, and to one side he fell
Smitten, and from his hand the cup outflew.
And from his nostrils a thick jet of blood
Sprang, as the table that beside him stood
He kicked aside and spurned away from him,
And on the ground was spilt the dainty food,
Bread and roast flesh gore-dabbled.

Book XXII, lines 1–21.

The Massacre of the Suitors

The Carnage

THUS THE LEADING SUITOR IS THE FIRST TO BE HIT, the first to be punished. Odysseus reveals his identity and declares he will take his revenge. Eurymachus tries to offer him compensation. When Odysseus refuses, he gives the signal to resist, but the hero's second arrow kills him. Telemachus kills the third leader, and goes to find weapons in the treasury. Unfortunately, he does not close the door properly, and the goatherd Melanthius manages to bring the suitors weapons to defend themselves with. Eumaeus catches him, ties him up and hangs him from the ceiling, but it is too late.

At this moment, Athene intervenes for the first time, in the guise of Mentor, but very briefly, only to *Give strength beyond his own for victory … essay / And of his glorious son.* Then she turns herself into a swallow and perches on a beam, diverting the spears of the suitors. It was more a massacre than a fight. Telemachus and Eumaeus are hardly scratched. On the other hand, the suitors go down in waves: Demoptolemus, Euryades, Elatus and Peisander, Eurydamas, Amphimedon, Polybus and Ctesippus, the sons of Damastor and Euenor.

> Thereat Athena from the roof on high
> Lifted her aegis that makes men to die,
> And scared their senses; and adown the hall
> They fled away, as herded cattle fly,
> That the quick gadfly drives in disarray
> In springtime when the long days are; and they
> As vultures with curved beak and crooked claw
> Swoop from the hills on wildfowl at their play,
> That on the plain skim low in hurrying flight,
> And these pounce down and kill them, and to fight
> No strength have they nor swiftness to escape,
> And men behold that hunting with delight:
> So these upon the suitors fell, and so
> Struck fiercely right and left amid the foe,
> And dismal was the clash of smitten heads,
> And all the pavement steamed with blood below.

Book XXII, lines 297–309.

The only ones to escape the massacre were the minstrel Phemius and the herald Medon. The former explains that he only sang under constraint, and that Odysseus would regret killing him: *Yourself a god you were, my song might be*. Odysseus is very attached to songs: we remember from his long tales in the palace of Alcinous how he wanted to hear the Sirens, and he had twanged his bow string like a good musician. The other man hid himself under a chair, and Telemachus speaks up for him. Once the men are punished, Odysseus calls for his nurse, Eurycleia.

And there she found Odysseus on the floor
Among dead corpses, splashed with grime and gore:
Even as a lion, having fed his fill
Upon a pasturing ox, moves on once more,
And all his chest and round by either jaw
His cheeks are smeared with blood, a sight of awe,
So blood-splashed was Odysseus, feet and hands. [...]
'O aged woman, let your heart be high,
But utter it not forth, nor raise the cry
Of victory: an impious thing it is
To triumph over men when slain they lie.
And these the doom of heaven has caused to fall,
And their own wicked deeds: for none at all
They reverenced of men that live on earth
Who came anigh them, were he great or small.'

Book XXII, lines 401–406, 411–416.

Until he was victorious, Odysseus kept his reason, and the moral he draws from this is the same as the poet gives at the beginning of the poem in the context of his companions, and that Zeus had repeated about Aegisthus: man is responsible for his own misfortunes as much as fate. The punishments are not yet over, however. Now Odysseus calls in the unfaithful servant women: they must wash the great hall, and then will be hanged: *Twitched with their feet a little, and so died.* Then it was time to wake Penelope. Eurycleia goes to tell her of Odysseus's victorious return, but the queen cannot believe such a thing: only the gods could do that. Even the nurse's mention of the scar does not convince her. She goes down, however, to see the dead and the man who killed them.

PRECEDING PAGE
The Death of the Suitors: The Odyssey, by Henry Moore (1898–1986). Perhaps the date this work was completed (1944) is significant. At all events, it admirably describes the carnage in the banqueting hall on Ithaca.

And now she gazed on him with all her eyes,
And now she knew him not through that disguise
Of the mean raiment, till Telemachus
Uttered a word and spake in chiding wise:
'O mother mine, ill mother, stubborn-souled,
Why from my father do you thus withhold
Your face, nor sit beside him and in speech
Make question and inquire that you be told?
No other wife might bear to leave alone
Her husband, thus returning to his own
After sore travail in the twentieth year:
But your heart ever is more hard than stone.'
Then answer made Penelope the wise:
'My child, the soul is dizzy with surprise
Within me; no word can I speak to him
Nor question him or look him in the eyes.
But if he comes indeed, and this is he,
We shall know one another certainly.
For we have tokens that from all men else
Are hidden, and none know but only we.'

Book XXIII, lines 94–110.

Penelope
and Odysseus

The Test of the Bed

Odysseus puts Penelope's doubts down to his unhealthy features and his rags. He encourages his son and supporters to wash themselves and, to deceive the people of Ithaca and avoid starting a revolution in the town, he asks the minstrel to sing a festive song, as for a wedding. The sound of the dances makes the townsfolk think that Penelope is finally about to remarry. Once Odysseus has washed and put on a fine robe, he returns like an immortal god to face his wife. Even this appearance fails to convince her, so much so that the hero asks for a separate bed be prepared for him.

'Fair mistress, sure beyond all womankind
The dwellers on Olympus have assigned
A heart inflexible to you; for none
Of women might endure with stubborn mind
From her own husband thus aloof to stand,
Who came to her and to his native land
After long travail in the twentieth year.
Up then, O nurse, and put for me in hand
A bed where I may lay me down apart.
Surely within her iron is her heart.'
And answering said Penelope the wise:
'Fair sir, I am not haughty, and no art
Of scorn is mine: nor much is it if so
I am astonished; and full well I know
What was your likeness, when from Ithaca
You started in the long-oared ship to go.
Now, Eurycleia, lay the goodly bed
Without the chamber firmly-established
That his own hands made: take it out from thence,
You and the women, and upon it spread
The broidered blankets, that he soft may lie,
And rugs and fleeces.' So she spake to try
Her husband: but Odysseus ill-content
Thus to his wife wise-hearted made reply:
'O wife, this word you utter likes me ill.
Who moved the bed? That were a feat of skill

Hard to perform, except a god himself
Coming removed it lightly at his will.
But of live mortals none, though young he be
And lusty, from its place might easily
Remove it; for a rare device was wrought
In the bed's framing, by no man but me.
Within our courtyard there grew spreading wide
An olive tree that flourished in its pride,
The thickness of a pillar in the stem:
Round it I built the chamber for the bride,
With solid stonework, and from roof to floor
Finished it well, and fitted in the door
Of close-set mortised planks; and afterward
The long-leaved olive's tresses off I shore;
And hewing square the tree-trunk where it grew,
I wrought it smooth with all the skill I knew,
Making it straight by line, and fashioned thence
A bedpost, and with augers drilled it through;
From the beginning I carved all the bed
With rich inlay of gold from foot to head
And ivory and silver, and across
I strained a leather strap dyed bright with red.
The token thus I tell: nor do I know
Whether my bed be still established so,
O wife, or some man have removed it thence
Cutting the stem of olive-wood below.'
So said he; and her soul and body grew
As water, when the token sure she knew
Told by Odysseus; weeping then she ran
Straight up, and round his neck her arms she threw,
And kissed his head and cried: 'Ah, hate me not,
Odysseus, seeing that wisdom you have got
Most of mankind in all things; but the gods
Wrought for us dole, being jealous that our lot
Should be to live together evermore
In joy of youth until we reached the door
Of age.'

Book XXIII, lines 166–212.

The Ingenious one thus finds his wife even more suspicious and wily than he is. Penelope wins from Odysseus what he has always carefully avoided: an instinctive reaction, a cry. She has broken the barriers behind which he for so long concealed himself. At the same time, she frees herself from so many years of constraint. The reunion is truly whole and complete.

The olive tree is the tree of Greece, representing a person's roots in their homeland, and it is often protected by rites. The fact that the bed was built round the olive tree and the house around the bed demonstrates with supreme clarity and delicacy the fundamental character of the sexual union of husband and wife, at the centre of their hearth and their land. It is a 'secret': a wonderful portrait of intimacy. This bed is irreplaceable, a symbol of faithfulness.

We see Odysseus as a craftsman on two occasions in *The Odyssey*. The first was when, in order to leave Calypso's island, he had to build himself a raft. He made the conjugal bed and the raft that brought him home. *The earth seems welcome to the shipwrecked.* Odysseus and Penelope: two shipwrecked people emerging from the waves onto terra firma.

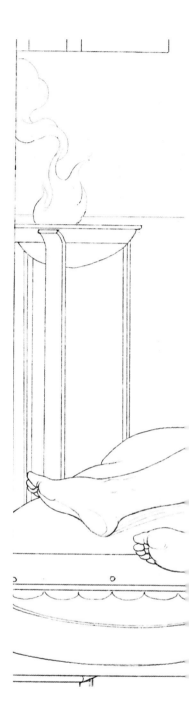

The End of *The Odyssey*

For the reunion of Odysseus and Penelope, Athene extends the night covering the world. The hero tells his wife that Tiresias has promised he will have yet more adventures. But finally they go to bed. The great conjugal bed is prepared. Eurynome leads them into the chamber, holding a torch: *When she had brought them their own roof below / Returned; and gladly then they sought the rites / Accustomed, and their bed of long ago.*

According to certain Alexandrian philologists, those lines marked the 'end' or the 'resolution' of the epic. Everything has in fact been accomplished. But the text handed down, which was known to Plato, contains seven hundred more lines, and a complete Book. There we read a second, very brief account of Odysseus's adventures as he described them to Penelope, the arrival of the souls of the suitors in Hades, where they meet Achilles and Agamemnon, the reunion of Odysseus with his father Laertes on his farm outside the town, and finally we learn how, faced with the threat of civil war in Ithaca, Athene forces a reconciliation between the families of the suitors and Odysseus.

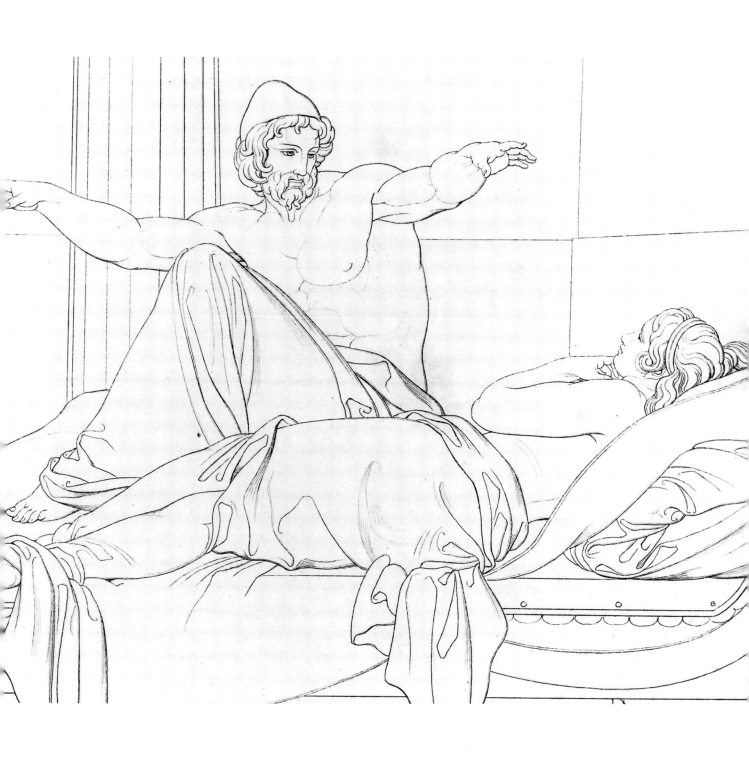

Odysseus and Penelope Share What
They Lived Through and Endured
during Their Twenty Years of Separation,
by Bonaventure Genelli
(1798–1868).

Characters in The Iliad and The Odyssey

The Iliad

THE TROJANS

Andromache
Daughter of Eëtion, King of Thebes, in Cilicia. Her father and seven brothers died in combat, killed by Achilles. Taken hostage after this battle, she was finally liberated for a ransom and married Hector, a Trojan prince. A loving and devoted woman, she embodies the family virtues. She gave Hector a son, Astyanax, who was killed by Odysseus during the fall of Troy. Andromache was captured by Neoptolemus, son of Achilles, who made her his servant and concubine.

Hector
Son of King Priam and Hecuba, the most valiant defender of Troy. His wife Andromache bore him a son, Astyanax. After killing many Achaean opponents, notably Patroclus, a great friend of Achilles, he died in a hand-to-hand fight with the latter.

Paris (or Alexander)
Brother of Hector, son of Priam and Hecuba. The gods chose him to decide who was the most beautiful, Athene, Hera or Aphrodite. He gave the golden apple of Eris (Discord) to Aphrodite. In return, the goddess promised him the love of Helen, one of the most beautiful mortals. Blinded by this love, Paris abducted Helen and precipitated Troy into war with the Achaeans.
Paris was chiefly remarkable for his beauty, and was not a courageous warrior. However, it was one of his arrows that, directed by Apollo, mortally wounded Achilles in the heel during the fall of Troy. He was in turn killed by Philoctetes.

Priam
King of Troy. Father of a large family (legend gives him fifty sons), he married Hecuba, his second wife, and with her had nineteen children including Hector, Paris, Cassandra, Polyxene and Polydorus. The Trojan War broke out during his reign, but his great age prevented him from taking part in the fighting. President of Troy's council, he gave the military command to his beloved son Hector. Overwhelmed by the latter's death, he

begged Achilles to return his body. He died at the hands of Neoptolemus, son of Achilles, when the Greeks took Troy.

THE ACHAEANS

Achilles
A demi-god, son of Peleus, King of the Myrmidons, and the Neirid Thetis, Achilles was a courageous warrior. Opposing the tyranny of Agamemnon, who used his power to take his favourite, Briseis, from him, he withdrew from the combat and left the Greek armies in a weak position. He refused the reconciliation offered by the King of Mycenae, and only returned to the fight out of desire for revenge when his great friend Patroclus was killed. He killed Hector and then, drunk with rage, defiled the body of the Trojan prince.
It was his fate to die on the Trojan battlefield. His mother Thetis knew this and tried everything to prevent the prophesy from coming true. As a child she had plunged him in the River Styx to make him invulnerable. His heel, remaining out of the water, was his only weak point. During the capture of Troy, Apollo, who knew of this weakness, directed an arrow there, fired by Paris, and this killed him.

Agamemnon
King of Mycenae, brother of Menelaus and husband of Clytemnestra. During the Siege of Troy, he was commander-in-chief of the Greek armies. Prepared to do anything to satisfy his ambitions and lust for power, he agreed to kill his daughter, Iphigenia, to guarantee the Greek fleet favourable winds on the voyage to Troy. He abused his power, behaving like an absolute monarch, and threatened the unity of the Greek camp. Achilles refused to bow to this tyrant's authority and threatened to withdraw.
It needed all the diplomacy of his advisors, notably Nestor, to convince Agamemnon to make honourable amends to the leader of the Myrmidons. The Greeks emerged victorious and Agamemnon returned as a conqueror to Mycenae. He had little time to enjoy his success: his wife, Clytemnestra, had him assassinated in order to seize power and avenge the death of her daughter Iphigenia.

Ajax
A gigantic man, endowed with great strength, he was the best Greek warrior after Achilles. Dressed in seven ox skins and armed with a bronze shield, this indefatigable colossus was in all the battles. On the death of Achilles, the arms of the King of the Myrmidons were to be given to the bravest of the Greeks. Ajax, convinced that he would get them, could not accept them going finally to Odysseus, deemed more worthy of them. Mad with rage, he massacred the Greeks' cattle before killing himself.

Briseis
This beautiful young prisoner was given to Achilles as part of his war booty after a victory before the Trojan War. She crystallised the discord between Agamemnon and Achilles when the former abused his power and ordered Achilles to give her to him.

Diomedes
King of Argos, he was one of the most valiant Greek fighters in the Trojan War. A companion of Odysseus in the long military campaign, he benefited from the support of the goddess Athene, who dressed his wounds when he was wounded by Pandarus and reduced his forces on the battlefield.
He was indefatigable and tenacious, never ceasing to encourage the Achaean troops in the fight. He refused to give up at moments of doubt and never retreated before any danger, not even when his enemies marched alongside gods such as Apollo and Aphrodite.

Helen
Fruit of the love of Zeus (turned into a swan) for Leda, Helen was famous for her great beauty. The wife of Menelaus, King of Sparta, she was used by Aphrodite, who gave her to Paris as a reward. He abducted her and took her to Troy. The Greek armies were sent after them, and set up siege around the ramparts of the city, thought to be impregnable until it was reduced to ashes.

Menelaus
King of Sparta, he demanded and won the support of his brother Agamemnon to recover his wife Helen, abducted by Paris to Troy. A man of no great character, he was neither a brilliant orator nor a distinguished warrior.

Once the Trojans were defeated, he returned to Sparta. The journey home took eight years. He was accompanied by Helen, the wife returned to him as a result of that bloody war.

Nestor

King of Pylos, in Messenia. He was very old when he took part in the Trojan War. Famed for his wisdom, he was much listened to. His powers of persuasion were not enough to reconcile Agamemnon and Achilles, but he convined Patroclus to put on Achilles' armour to repulse the Trojan assault. His young son, Antilochus, died in the fight. When the war was over, he went back to his kingdom of Pylos and ended his days there peacefully.

Patroclus

Patroclus was entrusted when young to the care of Peleus, and was brought up by the King of the Myrmidons like his own son, Achilles. The two young men grew up together, bound by a firm friendship. They set out for the Trojan War, but when Achilles refused to fight, Patroclus, wearing his friend's armour, took part in the battle to drive back the Trojans and was killed by Hector. Achilles, weighed down by grief, rejoined the battle with the Achaeans.

The Odyssey

Calypso

A nymph, daughter of Thetis and Atlas. She took in Odysseus when he was shipwrecked, cared for him, protected and loved him ... and kept him for seven years on her island. Odysseus dreamt of leaving and rejected the promises of immortality and eternal youth with which she enticed him. When the gods decided that Odysseus should return to Ithaca, Calypso protested but could not oppose the will of Zeus. She encouraged Odysseus to build a raft and advised him where to sail. She let him go with her heart full of tenderness and no bitterness.

Circe

Magician, daughter of the Sun and the nymph Perseis, she lived in a magnificent palace surrounded by forests full of men she changed into wolves and lions. She welcomed Odysseus and his companions and worked her magic on them, making them forget their homeland and then turning them into pigs.
Odysseus resisted, wanted to fight her and ended up as her lover after persuading her to turn his companions back into men. They stayed for a year on her island, then set off for Hades. After taking an oath of friendship, she showed Odysseus how to avoid the Sirens, and Charybdis and Scylla.

Eumaeus

Son of Stecios, King of the island of Syria in the Cyclades, Eumaeus was abducted as a child by pirates and bought by Laertes, father of Odysseus. Having become the royal swineherd when *The Odyssey* takes place, he was one of the few servants to remain faithful to Odysseus during his absence. He generously welcomed the hero on his return to Ithaca, without recognising him. When Odysseus revealed his identity, he embraced him in tears and helped him to confront the suitors by bolting the doors of the room where they were gathered, and where they fell one by one under the arrows of Odysseus and Telemachus.

Nausicaa

Daughter of Alcinous, King of Phaeacia. Thanks to Athene, who appeared in her dreams, she met and welcomed the shipwrecked Odysseus. The pure, beautiful girl told the hero to follow her at a respectable distance to her father's palace, where he was given splendid hospitality.

Penelope

Wife of Odysseus, mother of Telemachus. For twenty years she waited for Odysseus, away at the Trojan War. As his return was delayed, greedy suitors encouraged her to remarry so they could get their hands on Odysseus's kingdom. She misled them with a trick: promising that she would take a new husband when she had finished weaving Laertes's shroud, she unpicked during the night what she had woven during the day. Once they found out, the suitors, now installed in Odysseus's palace, were pressing her to choose a husband when *The Odyssey* begins.

Polyphemus

A gigantic Cyclope, son of Poseidon, the most savage of all the Cyclopes. When Odysseus and his companions landed on his island and got into his cave, he flouted the laws of hospitality and took them prisoner, then ate six of them. Odysseus made him drunk, he fell asleep and Odysseus used this chance to destroy his one eye before escaping. Furious at having been tricked, Polyphemus cried out in rage, begging his father Poseidon to punish Odysseus. The god of the Sea pursued the hero bitterly for years, preventing him from returning to Ithaca.

Telemachus

Son of Odysseus and Penelope. The first four Books of *The Odyssey* are devoted to him. As a child, he had to look on powerlessly as his mother's suitors pillaged his possessions. In his youth, the goddess Athene appeared to him disguised as Mentor and persuaded him to set off in search of his father. His adventures took him to Menelaus in Sparta, where he learned that Odysseus was a prisoner of the nymph Calypso. Back in Ithaca, he met Odysseus disguised as a beggar, hiding in the hut of Eumaeus the swineherd. Together they organised the massacre of the suitors.

Tiresias

Soothsayer from Thebes who kept his powers of divination up to his death. Odysseus met him in Hades and he foretold his future. In Sophocles, he revealed to Oedipus that he killed his father. He also advised Creon to bury Polynices and pardon Penelope, but in vain.

Odysseus

King of Ithaca, son of Laertes and Anticleia. One of the Achaean generals in the Trojan War, he led several difficult missions: he tried to negotiate the peaceful return of Helen, took Chryseis back to her father, gave courage to the Greeks who wanted to give up the siege, took part in the mission sent by Agamemnon to Achilles, organised the duel between Paris and Menelaus, and devised the trick of the Trojan Horse. He was as much a wise counsellor as he was a brave warrior. Chiefly, he is the hero of *The Odyssey*, which narrates his adventures on the long journey, strewn with pitfalls, that brought him home.

Further Reading

Homer and the Epic

AHLBERT-CORNELL, G. *Myth and Epos in Early Greek Art, Representation and Interpretation*. Jonsered, 1992.

BARDOLLET, L, *Les mythes, les dieux et l'homme, essai sur la poétique homérique*. Paris, 1997.

BEYE, C. *The Iliad, the Odyssey, and the Epic Tradition*. New York, Anchor Books, 1966.

BRUNET, P. *La Naissance de la littérature en Grèce ancienne*. Paris, Le Livre de poche, collection Références-Antiquité, 1996.

BUFFIÈRE, F. *Les Mythes d'Homère et la pensée grecque*. Paris, Les Belles Lettres, 1956.

CARLIER, P. *Homère*. Paris, Fayard, 1999.

COOLIDGE, O. *The Trojan War*. Boston, Houghton Mifflin Company, 2001.

FINLEY, M. *World of Odysseus*, New York Review of Books, 2002.

FORD, A. *Homer: The Poetry of the Past*. New York, Cornell University Press, 1992.

FOWLER, R. (ed.), *The Cambridge Companion to Homer* (Cambridge Companions to Literature). Cambridge, Cambridge University Press, 2004.

GRAVES, R. *Homer's Daughter*. Chicago, Academy Chicago Publications, 1982.

GRIFFIN, J. *Homer on Life and Death*. Oxford, Clarendon Press, 1980.

LAMBIN, G. *Homère le compagnon*. Paris, Éditions du CNRS, 1995.

LATACZ, J. *Homer*. Munich and Zurich, Artemis Einführungen, 1985.

LORD, A.B. *The Singer of Tales*. Massachussetts, Harvard University Press, 1960.

LUCE, J. V. *Celebrating Homer's Landscapes: Troy and Icatha Revisited*. New Haven, Yale University Press, 1999.

MADALENAT, D. *L'Épopée*. Paris, PUF, 1986.

MURRAY, G. *The Rise of the Greek Epic*. Oxford, Oxford University Press, 1960.

MURRAY, O. *Early Greece*, 2nd edition, 1993. Translated as *La Cité grecque à l'époque archaïque*. Toulouse, Presses universitaires du Mirail, 1995.

MURRAY, O., PRICE, S. *The Greek City: from Homer to Alexander*. Oxford, Oxford University Press, 1991.

PARRY, A. *The Making of the Homeric Verse*. The Collected Papers of Milman Parry. Oxford, Clarendon Press, 1971.

POURSAT, J.-C. *La Grèce préclassique des origines à la fin du vie siècle*. Paris, Éditions du Seuil, collection Points-Histoire, 1995.

ROMILLY, J. DE. *Homère*. Paris, PUF, collection Que sais-je? N° 2218, 1985.

VIDAL-NAQUET, P. *Le Monde d'Homère*. Paris, Perrin, 2000.

VERNANT, J.-P. *L'individu, la mort, l'amour*. Paris, Gallimard, collection Folio, 1996.

WOOD, M. *In Search of the Trojan War*. London, BBC Consumer Publishing, 2001.

WOODFORD, S. *The Trojan War in Ancient Art*. New York, Cornell University Press, 1993.

The Iliad

Translation

RIEU, E.V. Revised and updated by P. Jones, with D.C.H. Rieu. London, Penguin Books, 2003.

Commentary

KIRK, G. S. et al., *The Iliad, A Commentary.* Cambridge, 1985–1993, 6 volumes.

Studies

EDWARDS, M.W. *Homer, Poet of the Iliad.* Baltimore, 1987.

JOHANSEN, K.F. *The Iliad in Early Greek Art.* Copenhagen, 1967.

MAZON, P. et al., *Introduction à l'Iliade.* Paris, Les Belles Lettres, 1943.

MONSACRÉ, H. *Les Larmes d'Achille. Le héros, la femme et la souffrance dans la poésie d'Homère.* Paris, 1984.

NAGY, G. *Le Meilleur des Achéens. La fabrique du héros dans la poésie grecque archaïque.* French translation, Paris, Seuil, 1994.

OWEN, E.T. *The Story of the Iliad*, Clarke, Irwin & Co, 1966.

REDFIELD, J.M. *La Tragédie d'Hector, Nature et culture dans l'Iliade.* French translation, Paris, 1984.

REINHARDT, K. *Die Ilias und ihr Dichter.* Göttingen, 1961.

ROMILLY, J. DE. *Hector.* Paris, De Fallois, 1997.

SCHEIN, S.L. *The Mortal Hero: An Introduction to the Iliad.* Berkeley, 1984.

TAPLIN, O. *Homeric Soundings. The Shaping of the Iliad.* Oxford, 1992.

WILLCOCK, M. *A Companion to 'The Iliad'*, University of Chicago Press, 1976.

ZANKER, G. *Heart of Achilles: Characterization and Personal Ethics in the 'Iliad'*, University of Michigan Press, 1996.

The Odyssey

Translation

RIEU, E.V. Revised by D.C.H. Rieu. London, Penguin Books, 2003.

Commentary

JONG, I. DE *A Narratological Commentary on the Odyssey*, Cambridge University Press, 2001.

Studies

CLARKE, H. *The Art of the Odyssey*, Prentice-Hall, 1967.

DELEBECQUE, E. *Construction de l'Odyssée.* Paris, Les Belles Lettres, 1980.

GERMAIN, G. *Genèse de l'Odyssée.* Paris, 1954.

GRIFFIN, J. *Homer. The Odyssey.* Cambridge, Landmarks of World Literature, 1987.

HARTOG, F. *Mémoire d'Ulysse. Récits sur la frontière en Grèce ancienne.* Paris, 1996.

HÖLSCHER, U. *Die Odyssee, Epos zwischen Märchen und Roman.* Munich, Beck, 1988.

LOUDEN, B. *The Odyssey: Structure, Narration, and Meaning*, Johns Hopkins University Press, 1999

PAGE, D. *The Homeric Odyssey.* Oxford, Clarendon Press, 1955.

PUCCI, P. *Ulysse Polutropos. Intertextual Readings in the Odyssey and the Iliad.* New York, Cornell University Press, 1995.

SAÏD, S. *Homère et l'Odyssée.* Paris, Belin, 1998.

SCHEIN, S.L. (ed.), *Reading the Odyssey, Selected Interpretative Essays.* Princeton, 1996.

STANFORD, W.B. *The Ulysses Theme.* Oxford, 1968.

TOUCHEFEU-MEYNIER, O. *Thèmes odysséens dans l'art antique.* Paris, 1968.

TRACY, S. *The Story of the Odyssey*, Princeton University Press, 1990.

Index

Achilles: 7, 8, 10, 12, 16, 18, 21, 22, 33, 54, 58, 60, 67, 70, 71, 72, 75, 76, 78, 81, 82, 85, 86, 90, 92, 95, 99, 100, 102, 103, 105, 111, 112, 115, 195, 248
Aeacus: 71
Aegisthus: 125, 126
Aeneas: 90
Aeolia: 11, 175, 182
Aeolus: 11, 182, 185
Agamemnon: 8, 11, 16, 21, 22, 29, 33, 42, 58, 60, 85, 86, 111, 125, 248
Agenor: 39
Ajax: 33, 54, 67, 75, 106, 111, 195
Alcinous: 11, 13, 157, 160, 163, 166, 169, 171, 176, 195, 206, 216, 241
Alcmena: 132
Amphimedon: 240
Andromache: 49, 53, 54, 75
Antenor: 30
Anticlus: 139
Antilochus: 39, 75, 78, 81
Antinous: 129, 135, 237, 238
Aphrodite: 8, 34, 49, 64, 65, 166, 168, 169
Apollo: 8, 21, 67, 70, 72, 90, 95, 99, 103, 105, 160, 166, 232, 237, 238
Ares: 30, 38, 42, 46, 49, 85, 94, 112, 166, 168
Arete: 135
Argos: 11, 122, 139, 145, 220, 222
Ariadne: 87
Artemis: 154, 156, 160
Astyanax: 49, 53, 54
Athene: 8, 11, 12, 21, 38, 46, 99, 120, 122, 125, 129, 132, 136, 139, 142, 152, 156, 157, 160, 210, 216, 218, 237, 240, 248,
Atlas: 120
Atreus: 16, 18
Autolycus: 229
Briseis: 16, 21, 33
Calchas: 21
Calypso: 11, 122, 146, 148, 152, 175, 248
Cassandra: 142
Cebriones: 67, 81
Charybdis: 11, 96, 146, 175, 205
Chryseis: 21
Chryses: 21
Cicones: 11, 175

Circe: 11, 146, 175, 186, 189, 201, 205
Clytemnestra: 11, 125, 126, 169
Clytius: 30
Colchis: 175
Corfu: 175
Cronos: 58, 63, 70, 234
Ctesippus: 240
Cyclope(s): 11, 105, 146, 172, 175, 176, 179, 180, 181, 182, 232
Cythera: 175
Damastor: 240
Daedalus: 87
Deiphobus: 139, 142
Demodocus: 12, 13, 166, 171
Demoptolemus: 240
Diomedes: 42, 46, 58, 94
Dione: 49
Echepolus: 39
Elatus: 240
Elephenor: 39
Epeios: 142
Euenor: 240
Eumaeus: 11, 122, 208, 210, 213, 216, 218, 219, 220, 237, 240
Euphorbe: 70, 72, 75
Euryades: 240
Eurycleia: 122, 135, 226, 229, 232, 241, 246
Eurydamas: 240
Eurydice: 195
Euryloque: 186, 189, 201
Eurymachus: 237, 240
Gargare: 63
Hades: 11, 96, 103, 146, 189, 190, 195, 248
Hector: 8, 10, 18, 34, 42, 49, 50, 53, 54, 60, 67, 68, 70, 72, 75, 76, 78, 81, 85, 86, 90, 99, 100, 103, 105, 112, 115
Hecuba: 50
Helen: 8, 11, 16, 30, 33, 34, 53, 135, 139, 142
Hellas: 145
Hephaestus: 10, 63, 82, 85, 86, 90, 99, 166, 168, 169
Hera: 8, 21, 49, 60, 63, 64, 65, 67, 96, 168
Hermes: 122, 152, 166, 189
Hesperus: 100
Hicetaon: 30
Ida: 8, 58, 63
Ilion: 8, 10, 50, 56, 112, 220
Irus: 223

Ithaca: 10, 11, 12, 118, 122, 126, 129, 138, 145, 171, 176, 179, 182, 208, 216, 246, 248
Jason: 175
Knossos: 86, 87
Laertes: 12, 125, 130, 148, 171, 248
Lampus: 30
Laestrygonians: 11, 146, 175, 185
Laocoon: 142
Leto: 70, 156, 160
Libya: 175
Lipari: 175
Lotus-eaters: 11, 146, 175, 176
Lydia: 29
Maleia: 175
Medon: 145, 241
Melanthius: 218, 240
Memory: 12
Menelaus: 8, 11, 33, 34, 75, 122, 139
Menoetius: 68
Mentes: 122, 129
Muses: 12
Mycena: 132
Nausicaa: 11, 154, 160, 162, 163, 169
Neriton: 171
Nestor: 11, 58, 67, 75, 78, 81, 122, 136, 138, 139
Odysseus: 10, 11, 12, 29, 33, 58, 106, 111, 118, 120, 122, 125, 126, 129, 130, 135, 139, 142, 146, 148, 152, 156, 157, 160, 163, 169, 171, 175, 176, 179, 182, 185, 189, 195, 196, 201, 205, 206, 208, 212, 213, 216, 218, 219, 220, 222, 223, 226, 229, 232, 234, 237, 240, 241, 244, 246, 248
Olympia: 8, 12, 49, 120, 122, 168
Orestes: 125
Pandora: 138
Panthous: 30
Paris: 8, 30, 34, 54, 86, 103, 105, 142
Pasithëe: 64
Patroclus: 8, 10, 67, 68, 70, 72, 75, 76, 78, 85, 86, 100, 105, 106, 111, 115
Peisander: 240
Peleus: 8, 22, 78
Peloponnese: 135, 160, 175
Penelope: 11, 12, 122, 125, 126, 130, 133, 135, 145, 148, 152, 169, 218, 223, 226, 229, 232, 237, 241,

244, 246, 248
Perimedes: 201
Periphas: 46
Persephone: 190
Phaeacia: 11, 12, 135, 146, 160, 163, 175, 201, 206
Phemius: 12, 241
Phoenix: 58
Polites: 186
Polybus: 240
Polydorus: 90
Polyphemus: 105, 125, 172, 176, 179, 181, 182
Poseidon: 11, 60, 67, 90, 96, 125, 138, 152, 166, 179, 182, 229
Priam: 8, 10, 30, 33, 50, 53, 102, 105, 112, 115, 142
Pylos: 11, 122, 136
Sarpedon: 22
Scamander: 90
Scylla: 96, 146, 175, 202, 205
Sirens: 11, 146, 196, 201, 205, 241
Sleep: 64
Sparta: 8, 11, 122, 135, 139, 216
Sun: 7, 63, 146, 175, 205
Telamon: 106
Telemachus:10, 12, 118, 120, 122, 129, 133, 135, 136, 138, 139, 145, 208, 216, 218, 223, 232, 237, 240, 241, 244
Tenedos: 142
Thera: 87
Theseus: 195
Thetis: 8, 10, 22, 58, 81, 85
Thymoetes: 30
Tiresias: 189, 195, 248
Troy: 7, 8, 10, 11, 21, 22, 33, 49, 53, 54, 67, 105, 111, 112, 122, 125, 135, 139, 142, 146, 152, 168, 171, 175, 196, 201, 216, 222
Tydeus: 139
Tyro: 132
Ucalegon: 30
Xanthos: 90
Xanthus: 56, 90, 92, 96
Zeus: 7, 8, 11, 12, 16, 18, 21, 22, 29, 34, 45, 46, 49, 58, 60, 63, 64, 65, 67, 70, 85, 96, 99, 103, 115, 125, 138, 145, 148, 160, 166, 168, 172, 179, 181, 190, 206, 210, 213, 234

Photographic Credits

The Publishers would like to thank all those who cooperated on the production of this book, in particular Christelle Chevallier and Sophie Galibert.

Editorial director: Brigitte Leblanc
Art director: Nancy Dorking
Designer: Gaëlle Chartier
Layout: Séverine Morizet
Text editors: Myriam Blanc and Catherine Lucchesi
Production: Nicole Thieriot-Pichon

Photogravure: APS/Chromostyle, Tours

First published by Editions du Chêne, an imprint of Hachette-Livre
43 Quai de Grenelle, Paris 75905, Cedex 15, France
Under the title *Iliad et Odyssée*
© 2004, Editions du Chêne

English language translation produced by Translate-A-Book, Oxford

Text translations: William Marris, *The Iliad of Homer*, OUP, 1934;
J. W. Mackail, *The Odyssey*, Clarendon, 1932

This edition published by Hachette Illustrated UK, Octopus Publishing
Group Ltd.
2–4 Heron Quays, London, E14 4JP
English Translation ©2004, Octopus Publishing Group Ltd., London

ISBN-13: 978-1-84430-131-7
ISBN-10: 1-84430-131-1
Printed by Toppan Printing Co., (HK) Ltd.